the individual

TIME
LIFE
BOOKS

the individual

BY PAUL GOOD

AND THE EDITORS OF TIME-LIFE BOOKS

TIME-LIFE BOOKS, NEW YORK

The Author: Paul Good, a freelance writer and editor, has written a book, *The American Serfs*, on poverty in the rural South and dozens of articles for magazines such as LIFE, *Harper's* and *The Nation*. Most of his articles deal with society and the interactions of the individuals within it. He is also the author of a novel, *Once to Every Man*. He and his family live in Connecticut.

General Consultants for Human Behavior: Robert M. Krauss is Professor of Psychology at Columbia University. He has taught at Princeton and Harvard and was Chairman of the Psychology Department at Rutgers. He is the co-author of *Theories in Social Psychology*, edits the *Journal of Experimental Social Psychology* and contributes articles to many journals on aspects of human behavior and social interaction.

Peter I. Rose, a specialist on racial and ethnic relations, is Chairman of the Department of Sociology and Anthropology at Smith College and a member of the graduate faculty of the University of Massachusetts. His books include *The Subject Is Race, The Ghetto and Beyond, Americans from Africa* and *Seeing Ourselves*. Professor Rose has also taught at Goucher, Wesleyan, Colorado, Clark, Yale, Amherst, the University of Leicester in England, Kyoto University in Japan and Flinders University in Australia.

James W. Fernandez is Chairman of the Anthropology Department at Dartmouth College. His research in culture change has taken him to East, West and South Africa and the Iberian peninsula. Articles on his field studies have been widely published in European and American anthropology journals. He has been President of the Northeastern Anthropological Association and a consultant to the Foreign Service Institute.

Special Consultant for The Individual: Nathan Kogan is Professor of Psychology in the graduate faculty of New York's New School for Social Research. He is the author of *Modes of Thinking in Young Children* and *Risk-Taking, a Study in Cognition and Personality*, and has been consulting editor of *The Journal of Personality* and *Child Development*. Dr. Kogan is also a fellow of the American Psychological Association and is on the Board of Directors of the International Council of Psychologists.

Editorial Associates: Monica O. Horne, a member of the research staff of TIME-LIFE BOOKS, and Marion Buhagiar, a member of the writing staff, worked closely with the editors in the planning and organization of this series.

HUMAN BEHAVIOR
SERIES EDITOR: William K. Goolrick
Editorial Staff for *The Individual:*
Assistant Editor: Carole Kismaric
Text Editors: Virginia Adams, David S. Thomson
Designer: John Martinez
Assistant Designer: Marion Flynn
Staff Writers: Marilyn Daley, Suzanne Seixas
Chief Researcher: Barbara Ensrud
Researchers: Ruth Kelton, Fred Ritchin, Heidi Sanford, Lucy Voulgaris, Marie Schumann, Millie Swanson, Barrett Weeks

Editorial Production
Production Editor: Douglas B. Graham
Assistant Production Editor: Gennaro C. Esposito
Quality Director: Robert L. Young
Assistant Quality Director: James J. Cox
Copy Staff: Rosalind Stubenberg (chief), Charles Blackwell, Eleanor Van Bellingham, Florence Keith
Picture Department: Dolores A. Littles, Martin Baldassari
Traffic: Feliciano Madrid

Valuable assistance was given by the following departments and individuals of Time Inc.: Editorial Production, Norman Airey; Library, Benjamin Lightman; Picture Collection, Doris O'Neil; Photographic Laboratory, George Karas; TIME-LIFE News Service, Murray J. Gart; Correspondents Ann Natanson (Rome), Margot Hapgood and Dorothy Bacon (London), Maria Vincenza Aloisi and Josephine du Brusle (Paris), Helga Kohl (Athens), Elisabeth Kraemer (Bonn), Traudl Lessing (Vienna), Lucretia Marmon and William Marmon (Jerusalem), Robert Kroon (Geneva), John A. Callcott (Geneva), S. Chang and Frank Iwama (Tokyo), Mary Johnson (Stockholm) and Sue Masterson (The Hague).

Contents

A Face in the Crowd

1

Pick a high vantage point at noon in any great city of the world and watch the multitudes of human beings as they throng the streets. They surge, anonymous and energetic as neutrons inside an atom, flowing close and veering apart, a random concentration of bipedal creatures. The color of the teeming mass will change if the observation post shifts from Chicago to Djakarta or Accra or Peking, but the commonality of its appearance will not. Yet if an observer descends to the street and there studies close up the components of the crowd, scanning the bodies and staring into faces, he will be struck not by commonality but rather by variation—the individuality of each being within the mass.

Whether the crowd is white or black or yellow, he will see faces that are keen, dull, joyous, anguished, generous, rapacious, meek, threatening. And if he happens to glance at the reflections of people mirrored in a shop-window and perceives his own face among them, he may be reminded that however numerically great mankind is, it is ultimately a collection of individuals like himself, each one concentrated on his own destiny, bearing his personal perceptions and preoccupations, impelled by a vivid, unique sense of private personality that may be submerged by the crowd but is never lost in it.

This is the paradox of the human condition: people are at once much the same yet altogether different. The laws of biology see to that, guaranteeing distinctiveness from the moment a human begins to be formed. Before any individual can be born, a man and woman must meet and mate. Whether the mating occurs in a Park Avenue apartment, a thatched hut in a South American rain forest or a nomad's tent on a Mongolian plain, the man will provide some 300 million sperm cells, each packed with its submicroscopic load of heredity-controlling genes that transmit his own characterisitics in particular and those of his race and of the human species in general. No two men in the world produce sperm with the same configuration of about 30,000 genes in each cell, one of which will win the race to the egg. The woman's ovum, in turn, offers its inimitable 30,000 genes, ready for commingling with the sperm's. The different arrangements of the genes resulting from this genetic roulette are infinite, guaranteeing that the child will not be exactly like either parent, and certainly not like anyone else. Out of such odds as these emerge future plebians and patricians, Democrats and Republicans, lunatics and lovers.

Which they will become may depend partly on events that get underway with conception. For conception signals the start of the interplay between heredity and environment that will continue throughout each individual life. Genes release growth instructions to cells that multiply at an astounding rate. Four weeks after conception, the heart first starts to beat. At three months, minuscule fingers are flexing. By five months, the fetus has at least 12 billion nerve cells alone. But outside factors can affect and sometimes cripple the genetic potential. A mother's alcohol or drug intake, her illnesses and her diet all can limit development of the fetus. German measles in the mother can blind or deform an infant, and it is strongly suspected that her malnutrition—either ordained by poverty or created by slimming diets—can retard a baby's weight, and then its mental growth. In England, Nevil Butler of the University of Bristol studied 17,000 persons born during the same week in 1958. He found a consistent link between low birth weights and later difficulty in reading, number work and copying simple designs.

"If I were going to be a baby and could choose my Mum," Butler said, "I would have one about 25 in age, 5-feet-5 or taller, a bit plump, but with a normal blood pressure, a nonsmoker and from the upper classes."

The "upper class" requisite was not included out of snobbery. Other studies have indicated that well-fed upper-class mothers with high caloric intake (and sensible weight-control diets) can provide their children with a better, long-term nutritional lease on life than lower-class mothers. Bacon Chow, Professor of Biochemistry at Johns Hopkins University, found that schoolboys from poor families required more food to maintain growth than boys from rich families—even when both groups lived and ate together. The reason? Chow suggested that the mother's diet during pregnancy and lactation could affect the growth of her children, regardless of what they were fed later.

What is known about German measles in a pregnant mother, and strongly suspected about inadequate diets, leads to speculation about maternal emotions, disturbed or composed, and the benign or malignant marks they may leave. Who can say how many potential Shakespeares, Einsteins or Martin Luther Kings were the unfulfilled victims of an underprivileged prenatal environment?

The number of genetic and environmental possibilities is so great even before birth that no one can itemize all the ways in which humans may differ, let alone understand them. Individual differences can be grouped, however, in categories that illuminate behavior. Promptly at birth, people are divided from their fellow beings by physical characteristics. The largest and most obvious of these human dividers are the major differentiations of sex and race.

Perhaps the single most dramatic human difference is sex. Sex is determined at conception by genes grouped into two chromosomes, called X and Y, in the man's sperm. One of these chromosomes combines with an X chromosome from the mother. No one can predict which one it will be, but if the combination works out XY, the baby will be a boy; if XX, it will be a girl. The chances of being born an XY are slightly better than those of being an XX, male births outnumbering female ones by the narrow margin of about 104 to 100. But once the child is born, the chances of survival are better for girls than for boys.

The sexual difference has a number of important consequences on later behavior. Boys are more restless than girls, and more unpredictable. They start more fights, make more noise, take more risks, think more independently, are harder to educate and, contrary to most people's belief, are more fragile than girls and more vulnerable to a variety of diseases—including rickets, blood-clotting disorders and color-vision defects. They are also more likely to stutter, to encounter reading problems and to develop emotional quirks of all kinds.

Baby girls, on the other hand, are more robust than boys, but generally seem more dependent, submissive and conforming and less adventurous. They sleep more, cry less and demand less attention.

Over the years a broad spectrum of tests have sketched these and other sexual differences. Which of these are inherent, inevitable results of an individual's physical sex, and which are the consequences of training imposed by society's response to the person's sex, is much argued. There is no doubt, for instance, that career choices are influenced by cultural conditioning and male bias in a way that restricts women and curtails their rise in the professions. In Western societies little girls are traditionally encouraged to play with dolls and act out motherhood roles, to dream of becoming nurses and schoolteachers. Other jobs, such as those of secretary or telephone operator, are also traditionally female, although in recent years there has been a slight broadening of career possibilities. The little boy, on the other hand, is prepared for different roles; it is no surprise that in childhood's sexual game of doctor, he is the examining physician while the little girl plays the subservient role of nurse or the even more passive part of the juvenile doctor's patient. Boys still receive trucks, chemistry sets, footballs and—though many adults lament it—guns for Christmas. Many parents have come to appreciate the effects of such emphatic sex stereotyping of playthings; nevertheless, life directions are often clearly pointed under the Christmas tree.

But there can be no argument that even the careers of men and women are influenced by real differences in behavior. They seem to reside in the details of behavior rather than in broad, general aspects. Overall intelligence, for example, appears to be evenly distributed between men and women. Hundreds of comparative intelligence studies have been conducted on groups of females and males. One of the most extensive was conducted in 1939 by the Scottish Council for Research in Education. All of the children born in Scotland on four chosen days of the year 1926 were given the widely used Stanford-Binet IQ examination (Chapter 3).

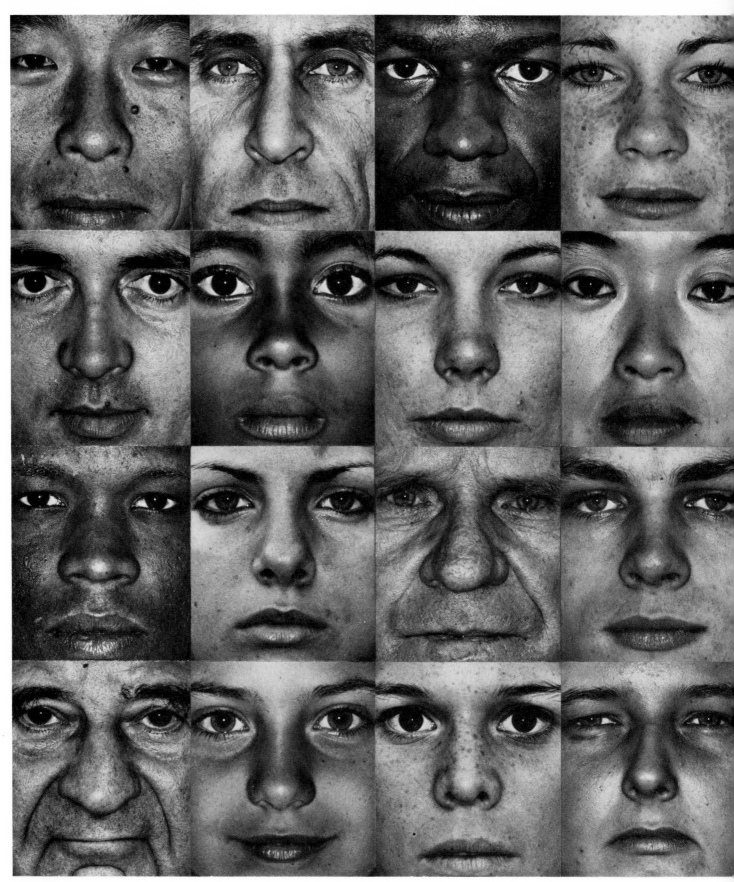

The physical differences that make a face unique are mirrored in these photographs by Ken Ohara. Even with hairlines, ears and chins

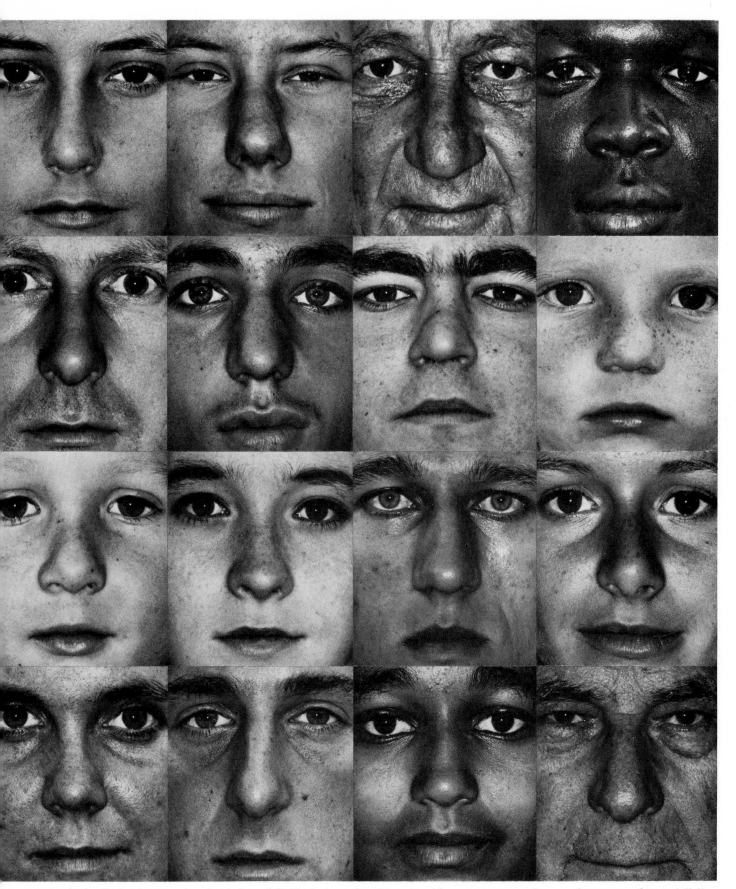

omitted, the distinctiveness of each of these individuals is made evident in wide or narrow eyes, long or short noses, thin or full lips.

There was no measurable difference between the boys and the girls.

When experiments examine more specific elements of behavior, however, they have no difficulty in isolating clear distinctions between the sexes. Females score consistently better in numerical computation and verbal fluency—breadth of vocabulary and facility in speaking and writing. Males show better arithmetical reasoning, more readily perceiving the principles involved in a problem. Women score higher in manual dexterity, men in speed and coordination of bodily movements.

The behavioral distinctions that can be seen in sex are not so apparent in the second great divider of human beings, race. Clearly, there are physical differences between the races. These distinctions presumably derive from "gene pools" gathered and transmitted over the years so that they become concentrated in people clustering together more or less exclusively. No one would mistake a Senegalese black for a fair-skinned Netherlander. Differing skin color has probably evolved in response to climatic conditions. In sunny, tropical areas the pigment-forming cells in the skin manufacture more melanin, which blocks ultraviolet rays from the sun, and thus protects the cells from overdoses of ultraviolet. The result of this pigmentation is dark skin. Fair skin, on the other hand, may be an advantage in temperate regions. Its relative lack of melanin permits absorption of greater quantities of ultraviolet from the weak sun, stimulating the skin's synthesis of vitamin D, which is essential to normal development of bones and teeth.

While racial differences mean differences in appearance, even these external distinctions among races and their ethnic subgroups are not so consistent as most people think. The noted anthropologist Ruth Benedict has pointed out that although Swedes are commonly thought of as fair-skinned blonds with blue eyes, studies of thousands of Swedish Army recruits showed that only 11 per cent possessed all three of these characteristics. Many Swedes, the studies showed, are brown-eyed, dark-haired and swarthy, or exhibit these supposedly non-Swedish characteristics in combination with those of the idealized Swedish "type." One of the most blatant—and ironic—attempts at stereotyping in recent times occurred in Nazi Germany when propaganda chief Joseph Goebbels extolled the tall, blond, muscular "Aryan" super race of Hitler's Third Reich. (Goebbels himself was short, slight and dark.)

How far racial differences extend beyond physical appearance has been an incendiary subject throughout history. Most recently, some people have revived the old charges that accuse some races of inferior intelligence—at one time or another such statements have been made about whites, blacks, Asians and, in the United States, about Indians, Puerto Ricans and other minority groups. Most experts accept the view stated by the Nobel Prize-winning geneticist H. J. Muller: "In regard to really important characteristics, the natural differences between the races pale into insignificance beside the natural differences between individuals."

The uniqueness of the individual is shaped by many factors: some, like race and sex, are obvious, but some are not. People are sifted, sorted and subdivided by their general physical appearance, fatness or thinness, tallness or shortness, the sounds of their voices, and such fine physical details as footprints and fingerprints. Finally, these distinctions are certified by a personal name, which becomes merged with the bearer's identity and to which he alone responds.

Such physical attributes are important aspects of individuality. They enable a person to be recognized by his friends; they are accepted as positive legal identifications and they also shed some light on behavior. Certain detailed physical characteristics such as hormonal concentrations may even explain why one man weeps when another laughs.

The very shape of the body itself is widely believed to reveal the person within. In Japan the twin pseudo sciences of physiognomy and metoposcopy have long flourished. Both are concerned with the reading of people's characters from a number of different facial features and bone structures. Round, thick ear lobes are held to be indicators of good luck and wealth, while a jutting jaw is thought to be a sign of a strong will. The Japanese also have a saying that "wisdom cannot fill up a large body," meaning that excessively tall people are likely to be fools—and yet extreme shortness is also regarded as a sign of stupidity or weakness, although less so in women than in men.

Though a large body is suspect in Japan, fatness is widely respected. An oversized stomach is thought to be a sign of magnanimity, and a man who speaks frankly is said to be talking from an open stomach. There is an old tradition that the abdomen is the site of the soul, and one who commits hara-kiri—suicide by disembowelment—is believed to have cut out his very essence.

In England a somewhat different attitude prevails. Fat people have long been assumed to be relaxed and jolly (remember Shakespeare's character Falstaff) and muscular but thin ones (like Hotspur) to be nervous, ambitious and temperamental. In the United States a Harvard scientist, W. H. Sheldon, aided by a number of associates, attempted to refine such observations about the relationships of physique to behavior and sought to put them on a scientific basis. In a long-range study of thousands of volunteers, Sheldon divided his subjects into three broad "somatotypes." First came the endomorphs, with soft, rounded bodies, weak in bone and muscle structure. Sheldon's study suggested that endomorphs were generally pleasure-loving, sociable, relaxed, big eaters and good sleepers. Then there were the hard and muscular mesomorphs, who seemed generally athletic, aggressive, dominating and extroverted. And finally came the ectomorphs, characterized by Sheldon as tall, thin and relatively fragile, inhibited, intense, introverted—and insomniac.

It is at once obvious that these classifications tell us what popular wisdom already "knows": fat people are genial and inert, rugged men make good soldiers and athletes, artists and thinkers tend to be wispy and moody.

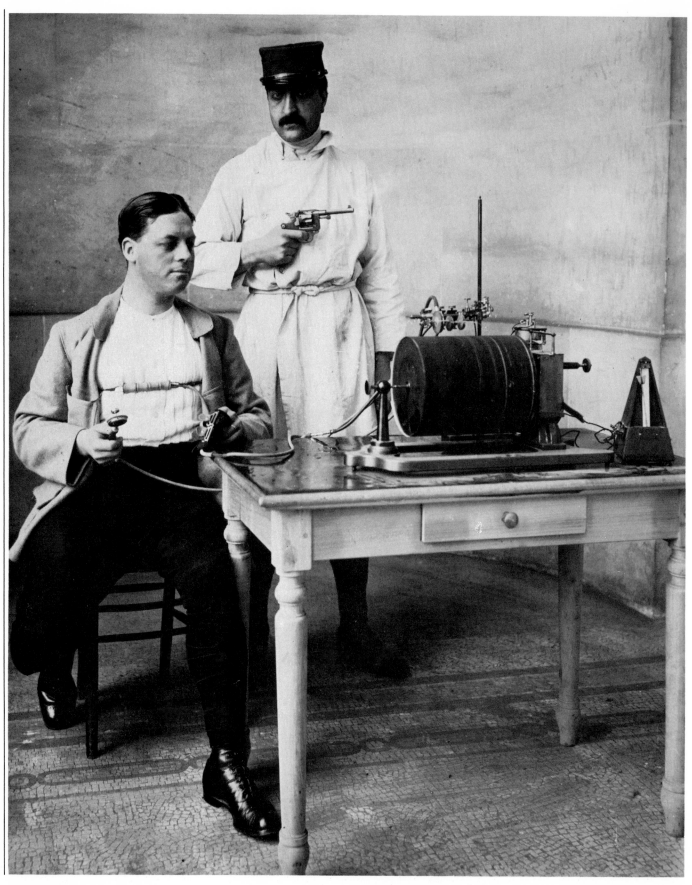

Tests to determine differences in individual physical reactions were invented in the 1880s and rapidly grew elaborate. This test, used in France during World War I, checked physical reactions of a prospective aviator. He was hooked up in a chest harness and given some gadgets to press. A pistol was fired by the kepi-hatted officer, and—if the subject survived and the apparatus worked—his heartbeat, blood pressure and muscle tension were measured.

It is equally obvious that exceptions, ranging from the sublime to the ridiculous, abound: the artist Picasso with the sturdy body of a bullnecked peasant; Hollywood endomorph Oliver Hardy, the ecto-meso soul of domineering crankiness.

Sheldon's study has served chiefly to embed the terms endomorph, mesomorph and ectomorph firmly in the language, but there is little doubt that body types have a definite effect on people's conceptions of others and themselves. The fact is that these physical factors may predispose a person toward certain behavior, which life experience may then systematically reinforce. Take the hypothetical case of three young male playmates, one fat, one thin, one medium. In their rough-and-tumble play, the medium boy consistently overwhelms the thin one and outlasts the fat one. Fat and thin are forced to make tactical survival choices. Thin may put a premium on agility, both physical and mental, to equalize his relations with medium, learning in the process how to retreat or withdraw psychically. Fat finds himself more adept at the less-arduous tactic of feigning lack of interest in youthful competition and consequently adopts the complacent role of good-natured observer. Meanwhile, the mesomorphic medium's belief in the use of aggressiveness to get his way is reinforced by the behavior of both playmates.

The physical uniqueness of every individual is obvious in external appearance, and it is confirmed by countless internal workings of the human body and mind, some of them readily observable, and some obscure. This essential fact of internal uniqueness was confirmed in mysterious fashion toward the end of the 18th Century by a seemingly trivial episode at Britain's Greenwich Astronomical Observatory, an episode that seemed at the time to be nothing more than a personnel problem.

David Kinnebrook, assistant to the Astronomer Royal, was rather unceremoniously fired because his timing of star movements—based on visual observation—differed from his boss's, sometimes by nearly a second. It was no comfort to Kinnebrook that 20 years later the German astronomer and mathematician Friedrich Wilhelm Bessel became intrigued with the timing discrepancies while reading a history of the Greenwich observatory and wondered whether perceptual differences between the two observers might have accounted for it. Bessel checked comparative timings with other astronomers and found that this was the case. There were substantial variations among individuals in terms of the speed with which they reacted to visual stimuli. Bessel called this difference "the personal equation." He might well have called it individuality.

The physical differences that distinguish each individual are repeated in every organ of the body, from brain size and shape to glands and their secretions. Tests on some 1,500 American soldiers showed a remarkable range in lung capacity, extending from below 96 cubic inches to more than 275 cubic inches. Experimenters have found a 60-fold difference in the amount of uric acid secreted in saliva, while the presence of a single he-

The lanky Masai's elongated frame provides a built-in cooling system. Because the human body is cooled by evaporation of sweat, the more skin surface, the faster heat is lost; the Masai's relatively great skin area helps him stand East Africa's heat.

Features ordained by climate

Some of the physical differences that distinguish one human from another may have developed as adaptations to climates in which modern man's forebears lived. Anthropologists theorize that the tightly curled hair of some tropical peoples emerged to protect the head from heat and the Tibetans' sparse facial hair evolved because a beard would freeze against the face.

Physiques also vary with the climate. Races from hot regions developed long slender limbs and slight torsos that cool their bodies efficiently, while Arctic peoples have stocky figures that retain heat. Skin colors, too, may possibly have been determined by the body's need to absorb enough—but not too much—vitamin D from sunlight.

Environmental influence is not easily unscrambled from the effects of migrations and ethnic mixing. But the pictures here are reminders that environment may have prompted the varied development of man's physical features.

The Eskimo's eye fold, a fatty layer under the upper lid of the eye, evolved to provide protection against sub-zero temperatures. The padding narrows the eye to a slit, to protect vision against glare and prevent the Eskimo's eyeball from freezing.

The size of this Jordanian's high-arched nose is functional, for by the time the dry desert air he breathes reaches the delicate inner surface of his lungs, it has been well humidified by the water in the moist membrane that lines his long nasal passages.

reditary factor makes the chemical agent phenylthiocarbamide taste bitter to some but tasteless to those lacking the factor. The psychologist Gordon Allport pointed out: ". . . the patterns of facial nerves are about as different as the river systems on different continents. About 15 per cent of people have no direct pyramidal nerve tracts. Some individuals have the sciatic nerve so embedded that it is well protected, whereas in others it is relatively exposed."

These details of physical variation may become critical in parts of the body's hormonal system, such as the endocrine glands, whose output of biochemical stimulators and inhibitors can control the quality—even the continued existence—of life. One endocrine gland, the pituitary, which resides at the base of the brain and controls growth, among other things, may vary greatly in production of essential hormones from individual to individual. Since the pituitary secretions set the rate of an individual's growth, the gland's output may determine whether an individual is puny and weak or big and strong.

The pituitary also affects another member of the endocrine gland system, the thyroid, which is located in the upper chest cavity and regulates the body's metabolic rate—the speed and intensity with which the entire human physical system operates. One person might have a brilliant mind and still accomplish little if his thyroid was underactive, condemning him to lifelong lethargy. Another might be driven to impatience, irritability and nonstop activity by a hyperactive thyroid. Some experiments have even shown that disorders of the thyroid gland can make people behave like psychotics.

Continuing research into the delicate chemistry of the human body is revealing more details of hormonal influence on behavior. The concentrations of certain hormones can determine whether a person is dour or cheerful, calm or irritable, energetic or listless. Other chemicals can affect sexual appetite. Still others in the brain make the difference between depression and euphoria, aggressiveness and timidity. Findings such as these come from the very forefront of research into the physical differences among individuals, and they promise eventually to provide a fundamental biological basis for the understanding of human behavior. They have not as yet done so.

Physical characteristics, no matter how detailed, do not offer many clues to the broader, and perhaps more important, attributes of behavior. They do not tell why the same person may be regarded by some people as brave, kind and sincere, but may appear to others as craven, mean and unreliable. Nor do they shed much light on the abilities that have enabled certain individuals to crack the atom, erect magnificent bridges or compose great masterpieces of art and music.

Each person's behavior is the product of intelligence, creativity, personality and adaptability, qualities that set men as a group apart from other animals and that account for the most substantial and significant differences among individual humans. It is these qualities that hold the key

Physical differences: a view from the nursery

Individual physical attributes—stoutness, thinness, or the size and shape of a nose—are noticed and commented on, often cruelly, from childhood. This juvenile tendency is revealed not only in the street calls of children, but in the works of writers and in nursery rhymes. Some examples are presented below. All poke fun at physical distinctions—except for the lesson in tolerance at left below, which Englishman Edward Lear wrote to go with his drawing above.

There was an Old Man with a nose,
Who said, "If you choose to suppose
That my nose is too long,
You are certainly wrong!"
That remarkable Man with a nose.

Jerry Hall, he is so small,
A rat could eat him, hat and all.

As I was going to sell my eggs,
I met a man with bandy legs,
Bandy legs and crooked toes,
I tripped his heels, he fell on his nose.

Fat and Skinny had a race,
Ran around the pillow case;
Fat fell down and broke his face,
And Skinny won the race.

Go to bed late,
Stay very small;
Go to bed early,
Grow very tall.

Brass buttons, blue coat!
Couldn't catch a nanny goat.
All policemen have big feet!

to many of the enduring mysteries of life. How do people become what they are? Why are some people more intelligent than others? And why are some more creative? What forces of heredity or environment or both conspire to produce the contradictions and complexities of human personality? And finally, do people change as they go through life, or are their special qualities fixed from birth?

These are the questions that have marked the long search of man in quest of himself—his search for the mysterious causes that make each individual behave in his own unique fashion. The search can be traced from the earliest myths of antiquity to the modern scientific era, with its sophisticated research techniques and complex investigative equipment.

According to early Greek thought, men often acted as they did because they were made to do so by the gods. Soon, however, the Greeks developed the more subtle theory that men acted in response to internal drives, that they created their own weal or woe as they either acted reasonably or gave in to pride and passion. It was not until the 17th Century, however, that

the importance of external factors as a determinant of individual behavior began to be appreciated. The English philosopher John Locke insisted that man comes into the world bearing a mind that is a *tabula rasa*, a clean slate with no inherited abilities or knowledge written on it. What a man became, according to Locke, was entirely the result of experience, of interaction with the environment. Other thinkers took the opposite view, that men were programed by heredity in the womb, so that their resultant lives were merely the acting out of a script whose genetic structure reached back to the deeps of man's racial history.

Many scientists since have compiled studies supporting one or the other view, either that individual behavior is largely determined by heredity or that it is generally the product of environment. Most researchers today take a middle ground, holding that human beings behave the way they do because of some sort of interaction between heredity and environment. Psychologists and psychiatrists, biologists and physicians seeking to discover both why people share certain characteristics and why they also differ have learned a great deal about man by looking at him, so to speak, from the inside out. Their work has been buttressed by that of sociologists, anthropologists and other specialists who have studied mankind from the outside, analyzing experience and its effect on the individual.

In this century, it became possible for the first time to measure human intelligence with some accuracy. Potential for brightness or dullness often (but not invariably) can be assessed at an early age. It is even possible to identify some of the external factors that influence mental development and to outline steps that stimulate intellectual growth. The process by which a creative person creates now seems more understandable—and it appears to apply across the board to achievements in literature, art, music and science as well as to the more ordinary efforts of the average individual. Individual personality has turned out to be far more complex than anyone had supposed, but as the intricacies are revealed, it becomes possible to understand better how they interact and also how they are affected by circumstances. Perhaps the most is known about the development of a person—the stages by which he acquires from inheritance and experience the unique qualities of body and mind that make him his own man, unlike any other human being on earth.

Legions of testers, probers and analysts are at work, but nature yields her secrets grudgingly and a full understanding of individual behavior is still a long way off. "We know more about the atom than ourselves, and the consequences are everywhere to be seen," says Carl Kaysen, Director of the Institute of Advanced Studies in Princeton, New Jersey. There are two major reasons why behavior is such a puzzle. First, the behavioral sciences are very young compared with the physical sciences. The astronomer and mathematician Copernicus reordered the physical universe five centuries ago, but it was not until the early part of this century that Sigmund Freud began to unravel the mysteries of the mind.

Even more important than the late start in research is the great diffi-

Differences in physique that characterize humans may determine the course of their lives. Basketball players like Kareem Abdul-Jabbar are one example. Shown here being measured by a normal-sized tailor, Abdul-Jabbar is seven feet two inches tall. He once said of his height: "People try to put you through a thing because of it and you reverse it on them by going into basketball. That has to be an important part of my success."

JOHANN CASPAR LAVATER

Physiognomy: reading faces

The idea that a person's facial features reveal his temperament goes back to Aristotle, but it was not systematized into a pseudo science until the late 18th Century. At that time a Swiss clergyman named Johann Lavater, in a work called *Essays on Physiognomy*, claimed he could read a man's character in the shape of his profile.

These theories enthralled such notables as Catherine the Great of Russia and the German writer Johann von Goethe; fashionable people had their silhouettes cut for analysis, and Lavater became an international celebrity. At right are some of his drawings of physical types, with his descriptions of each one's character. A glance at his own profile *(left)* makes it easy to spot which of the drawings represents Lavater's concept of the hero.

culty in comprehending psychological—as opposed to physical—characteristics. Each person's race, blood type and fingerprints are invariable throughout a lifetime. Universal measures of height and weight, of blood pressure and respiration can be agreed on by researchers. But human behavior is highly variable, and there is no universal yardstick that all scientists can employ to measure intelligence, creativity and personality. The scientists themselves, however hard they try to be objective, are conditioned by their own life experience, as they strive to understand their fellow creatures. Moreover, these creatures will not hold still like cells under a microscope. They change over time, are contradictory, sometimes hide their innermost feelings and often are unaware of their own potentialities. Public and private personalities in one individual may seem grossly incompatible. The judge who takes graft, the minister who philanders, the milquetoast who murders are, unfortunately, familiar figures in every culture and every time. Anyone who doubts the strange subtleties that exist in individual behavior has only to ask himself how well he knows his closest friend. Can he predict how his friend will behave in all circumstances? The friend's integrity may seem beyond question. He would never rob a bank and he always pays his bills and personal debts. But would he cheat on his income tax or his expense account?

Without understanding of an individual's inner, hidden qualities, no one can ever be sure of that individual's potential—for good or for ill. A person who pursues an undistinguished routine career for years may one

"*Portrait of a musical person. The forehead and eyebrows less profound in thought than quick in concept. Little produced, much imagined. Intensity is particularly expressed in the eyes and eyebrows. The mouth suggests the peculiarly tender, soft, breathless quality of exquisite musical taste.*"

"*Who does not here read reason debased; stupidity almost sunken to brutality? This eye, these wrinkles of a lowering forehead, this projecting mouth, the whole position of the head, do they not all denote dullness and debility?*"

"*The countenance of the hero: active, removed both from hasty rashness and cold delay. Born to govern. May be cruel, but scarcely; can remain unnoticed.*"

day produce work of genius. A seemingly dull and withdrawn individual may, given the opportunity, emerge as a powerful commander. The history of mankind is filled with such stories—the stutterer who became Demosthenes the orator, the peasant girl Jeanne d'Arc who led a king's armies, the monk Gregor Mendel who discovered the laws of heredity in his monastery garden.

A classic example of hidden potential was a young Austrian boy who was so quiet and diffident in school that his classmates and teachers suspected he might be simple minded. His elementary-school headmaster assured his father that it made no difference what the lad chose as a profession because he would "never make a success of anything." He was expelled from high school on the ground that his "presence in the class is disruptive and affects the other students." Somehow despite this sorry academic record he gained admission to a technical university, where he compiled a decent but not remarkable record; he was not invited to stay on and teach, as outstanding graduates often were, but instead took a job as a Technical Expert (Third Class) in a patent office. Although he was liked by fellow workers he was not considered especially brilliant. Or sociable: he went home each evening to the poor, sparsely furnished rooms his low salary allowed and thought and scribbled. Yet Albert Einstein's scribblings outlined one of the most momentous scientific breakthroughs of this century, the theory of relativity.

Another example of a young genius whose potential went unrecognized

Physical appearances have long been interpreted by many as indicators of inner character, even though no such relationship actually exists. In "The Carrying of the Cross," painted by the Flemish master Hieronymus Bosch, the artist characterized the bestiality of the men who jeered Christ on His way to Calvary by giving them deformed noses, snaggled teeth and pop- or slit eyes.

until he was well into manhood was Charles Darwin, author of modern evolutionary theory. Darwin was born to wealth and exposed to the finest English education, although for a time he made little of it. His father once prophesied: "You care for nothing but shooting, dogs and rat-catching, and you will be a disgrace to yourself and your family."

Money and position enabled the mediocre student to take up medicine at the University of Edinburgh, and when he wearied of that, to transfer to Cambridge to prepare for the ministry. It was at Cambridge that he discovered his love of natural history, but he remained little more than a dilettante, collecting beetles and enjoying field trips. When a friendly botany professor suggested that Darwin go on the five-year, round-the-world scientific cruise of H.M.S. *Beagle*—at no pay—his father refused permission. But the very next day, young Darwin happened to go out shooting with a sympathetic uncle who thought well of the proposed trip. The uncle persuaded Darwin's father to let the young man go, providing Darwin the opportunity to observe how related animals had adapted in varying ways to varying conditions in their struggle for survival; he thereupon formulated the Darwinian theory of evolution.

Still another dramatic case involved a physically small, unprepossessing boy from an isolated old town in the American South. He was an indifferent student and never finished high school. Admitted to college despite the lack of a high school diploma, he promptly flunked out. He could not, or would not, hold a job, losing his appointment as postmaster because he spent more time reading and gossiping with friends than tending to the mail. After he was fired he announced that, "I will be damned if I propose to be at the beck and call of every itinerant scoundrel who has two cents to invest in a postage stamp." The combination of this arrogant fecklessness, a curious taste in clothes (sometimes knickers worn with bare feet) and a talent for loafing around the town's courthouse square earned him the nickname of "Count No'count." His real name was William Faulkner, winner of the 1949 Nobel Prize in literature and one of the greatest writers that America ever produced.

If profound wells of intelligence and creativity can lie hidden, so strength of personality may disguise itself only to be revealed later. Nobody who knew Eleanor Roosevelt as a gangling, buck-toothed ugly duckling of a girl ever dreamed she would become a great moral force in 20th Century life. Shy and withdrawn, especially after the early death from drink of her adored father, she married a glamorous cousin—only to find her household tyrannized by her mother-in-law and her relationship with her husband scarred by his infidelity.

Yet during Franklin Roosevelt's 13 years in the White House his wife's strong character emerged clearly. She operated as the polio-crippled President's eyes and ears—tirelessly attending functions, meeting people, seeing things, doing what he could not. She exerted powers given to no other President's wife, and after F.D.R.'s death the ugly duckling came to be known as the First Lady of the World, an honored and influential figure at home and abroad.

These are famous cases. More commonplace ones abound in every society in the world. Individuality continuously struggles to assert itself through four key attributes of human behavior: intelligence, the ability to reason and comprehend; creativity, the talent to make something that is original and worthwhile; personality, the complex of attributes that characterizes the whole person; and adaptability, the capacity for change. These fundamental characteristics are possessed in some degree by every human. The chapters that follow describe present knowledge of them, showing how science isolates and measures these characteristics, how each may be modified and enhanced and why individuality is so important.

Identical twins: alike but different

Thirteen-year-old Jean (left) and Jo Parks look so much alike that even their mother sometimes confuses them. For this picture the twins accentuated their likeness by wearing identical pigtails and cotton-jersey tops—an uncharacteristic match for sisters who usually insist on dressing as independent individuals.

The pert youngsters at left provide the ultimate test of individuality, for they began as one person and then divided in two—identical twins formed when a single ovum split into an identical pair soon after conception. Jean and Jo Parks, who live with their parents and older brother in Louisville, Kentucky, thus inherited the same genes and share the same genetically determined characteristics.

The Parks twins have the same hair and eye color, matching hairlines, skin textures plus pigmentation. Having been brought up together, the sisters have also had the common environment that tends to reinforce their hereditary similarities. However, in spite of all their alikeness and temperamental closeness, each is very much her own particular self.

The girls' differences were noted early when as babies they began to take part in a University of Louisville study of twins. Even then a researcher found Jean was jabbering and friendly but sensitive, while Jo was quiet, reserved and placid. A dozen years later, family and friends noted that the distinctions were clearer yet. Jean had a quick but not very intense temper, a happy-go-lucky tendency to slough off hurts and an imaginative restlessness that propelled her from one interest to another. Jo more often brooded over slights, analyzed her attitude toward people and focused her attention more sharply than Jean.

The girls themselves always insisted on their individuality. Asked by a new acquaintance, "How can you tell yourselves apart?" they shot back the answers: "Well, I certainly know who *I* am!" "And I know who *I* am!"

PHOTOGRAPHED BY
CHARLES HARBUTT

Closer than sisters

Jean and Jo Parks are a happy example of a finding in 1966 by Chicago psychologist Helen Koch that identical twins feel closer to each other than do any other siblings. The sisters share a room decorated out of matching tastes. On long car trips they entertain each other for hours by making up games.

The twins' compatibility is bolstered by common interests: fervent music lovers, they attend the Kentucky Opera Association's performances in Louisville, take piano lessons and sing in school and church choruses. And a mutual enthusiasm for animals sparks their current ambition to run a horse farm —together, of course.

Both animal lovers, Jean (left) and Jo give their grandparents' tired hunting dogs a lift.

Jo (left) and Jean learn a new song together while they loll companionably on the big, old-fashioned metal bed that they share.

Raising their soprano voices, Jo (left) and Jean sing along with others in the school chorus at a rehearsal for a Christmas program.

Jo, engrossed in her private world of books, reads Johanna Spyri's classic tale of a Swiss mountain girl, "Heidi."

One for reading, one for doing

Along with all their shared activities, each of the Parks twins pursues occupations on her own. These hobbies have developed out of distinct aptitudes that mark the sisters as separate personalities. Jo is an avid reader, devouring anything from Edgar Allan Poe horror stories to biographies and adventure novels. She excels in vocabulary tests and examinations that gauge abstract reasoning and the retention of information.

Jean is more of a doer. She scores well on visual tests that require coordination of eye and hand, easily finding tiny clues to complete a picture or organize objects into a pattern. She likes traditional feminine crafts such as embroidering, crocheting and knitting, but she is also good at woodworking (she built a bookshelf and a cat-carrier). Most of all she enjoys making things —burlap wall hangings, soap carvings, clay animals—that are novel and, because she is invariably impatient to see the results, quickly finished *(right).*

Jean, building a personal totem pole, wraps some paper around a stack of coffee cans.

*Ravenous at breakfast, a fully awake Jean
(left) digs into her pancakes, the
very sight of which seems to repel her
still-drowsy sister—who nevertheless is
the hungrier eater at later meals.*

Differing life styles

At home, where each girl has been allowed to follow her own bent—neither
has ever been pressured to "be like your
sister"—the Parks twins display temperamental contrasts. Jean is a morning
person who bounces out of bed as soon
as she is called, active and alert. Jo
drags herself up only after repeated ap-
peals, and stays groggy almost until the
school bus comes by.

Not surprisingly, Jo is the more re-
luctant to go to bed at night. Openly admitting her hatred of housework, she
spends hours dawdling over a dusting
assignment, while Jean does such tasks
both diligently and cheerfully.

*Jean pitches in to help her mother clean
the floor in the family room, while
Jo cavorts on the couch—one of several
delaying actions intended to put off
the moment when she, too, must help out.*

Engaged in carefree lunchtime chatter with a girl friend in the school cafeteria, Jean is oblivious to an interested gaze from a schoolmate of the opposite sex.

An interest in boys: stirring but unequal

At 13, both Jo and Jean Parks like boys, but Jo is more aware of them than Jean. She pays great attention to her appearance, works harder at attracting and holding notice, and will sustain her interest in a particular boy over a lengthier period of time.

Jean is less self-conscious and less flirtatious than Jo, yet enjoys an easy popularity with friends of both sexes. Still, she no less than her sister can get into a dither over male company. When their young male piano teacher was expected for a lesson, both girls changed clothes five times.

Jo, who is more demonstrative before the boys, enjoys the limelight as she shows off her prowess in using a muscle exerciser she has grabbed from one of them.

For these twins,
no twin fashions

When the girls were very young, the Parks twins' mother found that, try as she might, "at times it was hard not to lump them together if there they were in front of me, looking so alike." Often she dressed them identically.

But once the girls began dressing themselves, they developed a marked preference for different outfits. They sometimes wear matching clothes for a lark—usually novelty styles. But mostly they choose quite dissimilar clothes: for a trip to the ice rink, Jo wriggles into a velvet skating skirt, while Jean goes as she is, in an old shirt and jeans. In clothes, as in the choice of activities and friends, the twins' diverging tastes are a reminder that they are growing up alike but different.

Perched together on a roof, the Parks twins vaunt their climbing superiority over a small boy. Barefoot, pigtailed Jean (left) wears a bulky sweat shirt and flare-legged denims, as opposed to Jo's saddle shoes and hanging hair, flowered cotton smock and slim-styled pants.

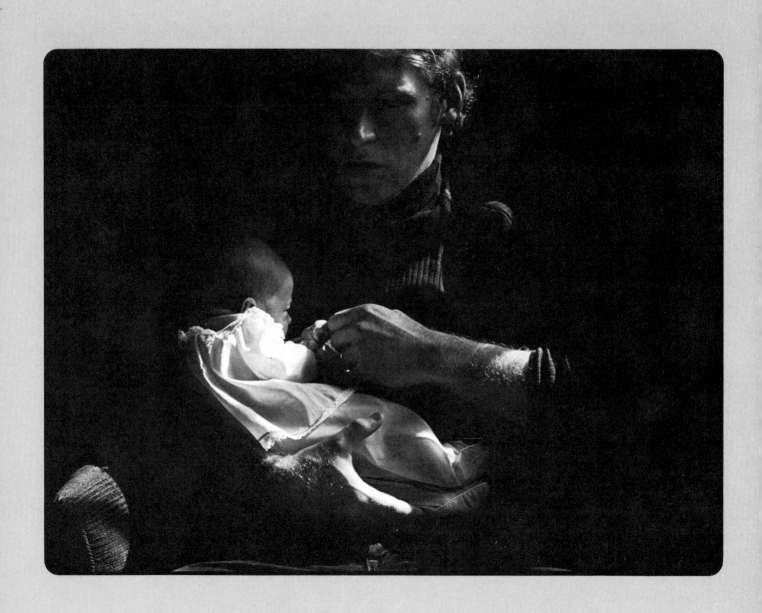

Father of the Man

2

A baby is born, sound and sassy. Its birth is a joyous reassertion of the old pedantic mouthful, ontogeny recapitulates phylogeny—the development of the individual duplicates the evolution of the species. So the infant, whose earliest ancestors came from the sea, takes a reverse plunge into life. Like a diver in old poolside movies run backward, the baby is ejected from the sea-like environment inside the saline amniotic sac and thrust into the dry world (which it subsequently dampens) of infanthood.

Although none can remember this entry, it is surely a traumatic experience, the ultimate in culture shock, what one psychoanalyst has called "the most total reorganization of a person's lifetime." Compared to the protective warmth of the womb, the external temperature is like a cold shower after a steam bath. The small lungs must suddenly work to provide oxygen heretofore gently piped in via the placenta. Among the assaults on the newly minted flesh is an invasion of microbes. The infant's insides are sterile at birth; within 24 hours, breathing, sucking and swallowing have introduced bacteria into the lungs and intestines and the baby is assuming man's ancient role of host to germs. But even as the child assumes its burden of recapitulating phylogeny (a large burden for something so small), the newborn is asserting something else—its inchoate individuality.

During the first few years of its life, the child develops with astonishing rapidity the attributes that will thereafter distinguish it from other human beings. The fact quickly becomes obvious to every parent, and the realization has been noted in a number of sayings through the years. The 19th Century poet William Wordsworth stated it metaphorically: "The child is father of the man." At least part of this individuality is inherited; "Like father, like son," goes the folk saying. Equally well established has been the idea that individual characteristics are drastically influenced by experience during childhood; a Jesuit maxim of the 17th Century claims: "Give me a child until he is seven and I will give you the man."

But it was not until the 20th Century that the mechanisms behind these hoary generalities began to be uncovered. Some of the links between heredity and individual characteristics have been found. Universal patterns of development have been sorted out. Science can advise parents at what ages different abilities may emerge. Family and environmental influences, ranging from brutal or indifferent parents to social deprivation, may impede or retard a child's development. Some psychologists argue, like those early Jesuits, that almost total molding of individual character is possible. They believe that rigid training from the cradle on could determine whether a child would grow up peaceable or aggressive, bohemian or conservative, kind or cruel. This view is extreme, the old nightmarish dream of man playing God and working human clay as a sculptor fashions figures. But few deny that the so-called formative years are just that—a critical period for the emergence of individuality.

It is sometimes difficult to appreciate this individuality at first. Consider the maternity ward where dozens of infants only a day or so into the world lie behind a glass partition in sleeping or squalling files. The babies assembled here may look different from one another, but the passing stranger would be hard pressed to spot their individual characteristics. Their sameness may pose a problem even for the obstetrician. The doctor is expected to comment on the particularity of the creature just delivered into his hands, to certify its uniqueness. One veteran obstetrician, who had delivered thousands of infants and in the process had run out of things to say, finally devised a standard family-pleasing observation.

"Well!" he would exclaim. "That *is* a baby."

The doctor's dilemma is understandable, for babies even act much alike as they pass from one stage of development to another. Many psychologists have studied the universal sequence by which human beings develop and individual differences appear. Subtle month-to-month, almost day-to-day changes were observed and catalogued by Arnold Gesell and his associates at the Yale Clinic of Child Development during the 1920s and 1930s. Studies like Gesell's constitute a universal script against which the performance of all emergent individuals may be measured.

Among the most helpless of all newborn animals, the human infant can cry but cannot find the nipple on its own. It cannot raise its head, and its eyes stare unfocused for long periods, although a flicker of response may reward a face bending over the crib.

By about four months, the universal baby first flashes the "social smile" in beguiling acknowledgment of a familiar face. It holds its head up and looks around, greatly increasing the scope of its world; it likes to sit in a lap or be propped up by pillows. Eye and muscle coordination are improving and it can hold a rattle. About three months later "ma" and "da" are heard, although true speech is still a long way off. By the end of the 10th month the baby waves bye-bye but often makes it yowlingly clear that it does not want to see people go.

In the year between one and two, the infant takes a giant step—starting with a crawl—from infancy toward childhood. It begins the year on all fours; still puppyish, it responds to commands to give up a ball. Before the year is out it will walk erect and issue commands of its own. During that transcendent year, the emergent individual is a dynamo of neural and muscular growth, a pint-sized, highly selective computer zealously storing intellectual and emotional inputs for the long haul ahead.

And so the drama of early development unfolds. Within the overall pattern of similar development, common to all the children everywhere, individual differences steadily emerge. Some infants blessedly sleep through the entire night; others demand nocturnal feedings from groggy parents. No matter how many blocks the development charts say a baby can pick up at age one, it may choose to pick up more, fewer or none at all. Joseph L. Stone and Joseph Church, authors of *Childhood and Adolescence*, pinpoint some of the key variations: some "babies drain their bottles in a single rush, others remain unhurried and even indifferent during a feeding. Some babies can hardly wait to become mobile, others seem content to stay comfortably in one place." While the average child has about 300 words at the tip of its tongue at the end of the second year, some have double that number. On the other hand, the British author Virginia Woolf, whose language talent made her one of the great literary figures of the 20th Century, did not speak a word until she was three.

Many of the differences that have been detected among infants are distinctive attributes of character and temperament that will probably mark the individual through the years. Some of these characteristics were investigated by Stella Chess, Alexander Thomas and Herbert G. Birch, who established a long-range behavioral study of 231 children from infancy into the teen years. This study found marked differences in such characteristics as the persistence or determination shown by newborn children. "We observed great variation in the ability of different babies to continue an activity in the face of difficulties or to resume it after interruption. Some children sucked very persistently at the nipple with small holes, even if little milk was coming through. Others gave up quickly. The persistent infant kept trying to reach a toy that was out of reach. The nonpersistent one tried for only a few minutes."

Chess noticed that this persistence, or lack of it, set a behavior pattern that continued as the child matured. "All children change as they grow older, but most of them continue in important ways during the later years to exhibit some of the qualities of behavior they showed in early life. . . . The child with a long span of attention gazed at his cradle gym intently for half an hour. The same baby, a year later, would stick with one toy for quite a long period. A baby with a short attention span, on the other hand, would focus only briefly on any activity or aspect of the environment. At a year and a half he might flit from toy to toy, spending very little time with any one of them."

One of the most persistent individualists in the Chess study was a very active boy who at 18 months learned to tie his shoelaces (at three, say the charts, children first learn to *un*tie them). He then proceeded to tie all the shoelaces in the house that he could lay his hands on.

The emergence of marked and persistent attributes so early in life—before outside influences can have much effect—is convincing evidence that they are innate, built into the child's heredity. It is more than a century

since an Austrian monk, Gregor Mendel, harvested laws of heredity from his plot of garden peas. Mendel bred plants selectively and showed how certain characteristics in the parent plants were passed on to the new ones. He was able to work out mathematically, for example, the probable color of the progeny when green and yellow peas were crossed. Some color traits were dominant and appeared very often, others were recessive and appeared infrequently; gradations between the two would occur according to predictable formulas. Similar simple rules trace the heredity of some human physical characteristics, such as eye color.

Scientists ever since Mendel have been investigating the genes and the ways in which they influence human development. Great breakthroughs have been made. The structure of the DNA molecules that carry the genetic coding is now understood. It is this coding that makes us all human, and yet all unique. But unfortunately, the precise functioning of DNA coding remains a mystery. Most information about it is limited to genetic malfunctioning in certain diseases: the royal curse of hemophilia, which causes prolonged bleeding; Tay-Sachs disease, which destroys the central nervous system and affects mainly Jews; sickle cell anemia, a blood-cell abnormality latent in two of every thousand American blacks.

Heredity's responsibility for normal traits is not so easily traced. The sickle cells in the blood of parent and child can be matched under a microscope, but there is no microscope that can spot the genes in a father and son that make them look or act alike. So far, and hopefully hereafter, human beings are not considered fit subjects for the kind of selective breeding that enables hereditary traits to be identified in animals. Even if some latter-day Dr. Caligari wanted to try it, humans make poor experimental animals for genetic research. To begin with, their gene pools are so hopelessly mixed in the mélange of interbreeding that it would take eons to breed anything resembling a "pure" type. Human generations take a long time to mature; a researcher quickly finds himself outlived. Human test animals are prone to contaminations like love and ambition. They are, to say the least, particular about how, when and with whom they will breed. Finally, their natural environment is our human comedy with all its interwoven complexities, which cannot be approximated in a laboratory and without which no experiment could claim validity.

So researchers, fashioning tools for use in determining how heredity may shape a human baby in its present and future, turn to humbler and faster breeding creatures—laboratory fruit flies, rats and mice, for example. The first few faltering steps with these animals upset some cherished theories. One of these experiments was inspired by the 19th Century French naturalist Jean-Baptiste de Lamarck, who propounded the view that physical characteristics acquired by animals during their lifetimes could be passed along to their offspring. A resolute researcher named August Weismann set out to test Lamarck's theory by cutting the tails off newborn mice and breeding these animals to see whether the bobtailed characteristic would be transmitted to succeeding generations. Thousands of sore tails

Individual attributes that may last a lifetime often surface early, as indicated by this pictorial study of a six-month-old girl's persistence. In the top row of the sequence (left to right), the baby reaches for rings suspended over her. After she hooks onto one (second row), a proffered toy dog is rejected and pushed away (third row). Given the dog one more time (fourth row), she again pushes it aside and, as the sequence ends (fifth row), she is still determinedly clutching the ring.

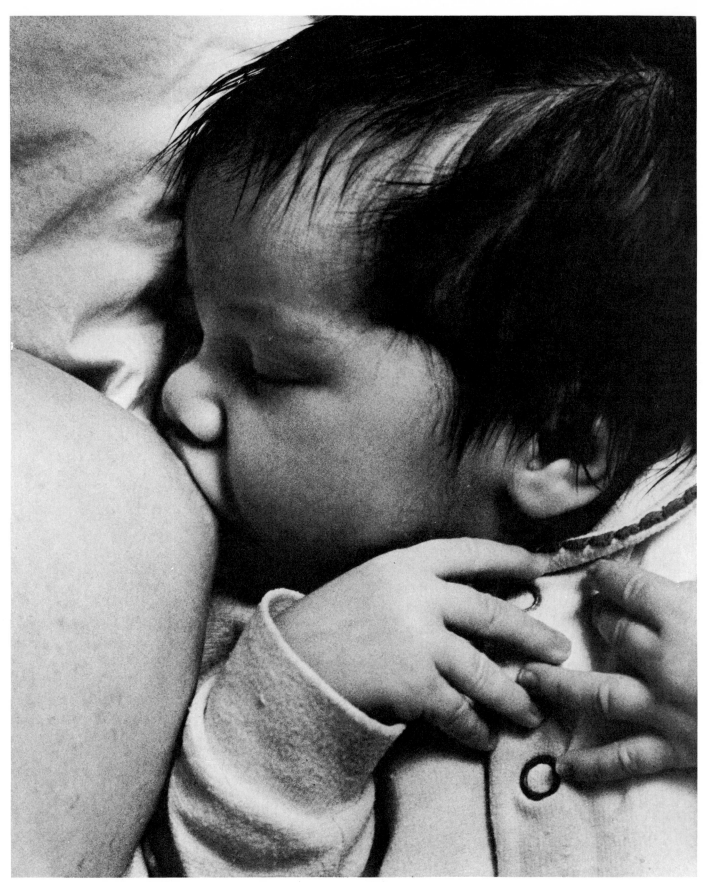

A baby nurses at its mother's breast, following its own special habit. This two-week-old prefers five or six sucks followed by a brief rest.

Scrutinizing his world, an eight-week-old focuses on a rattle, exercising a skill of all babies his age. But no two focus the same way.

Baby's unique ways

To survive the confusion of the new world around them, all babies come equipped with certain instincts, reflexes and perceptual abilities. But the development of these instincts and abilities and the ways in which they are used are a matter of individuality.

Every baby is born with the sucking instinct, which enables him to eat. But some babies suck almost all the time, while others are so indifferent that they frequently interrupt their feeding and take up to an hour to nurse.

Nearly all newborn babies are able to focus on objects up to eight inches away, and tests have found that they immediately examine any visual pattern. But the same tests discovered that some infants looked at the corners of a triangle, while others concentrated on two sides, and still others went over its entire surface. At birth all babies grasp a proffered finger so tightly they can support their bodies from it. There is little human need for this reflex and it vanishes early, but when it vanishes may vary from around three to 12 weeks.

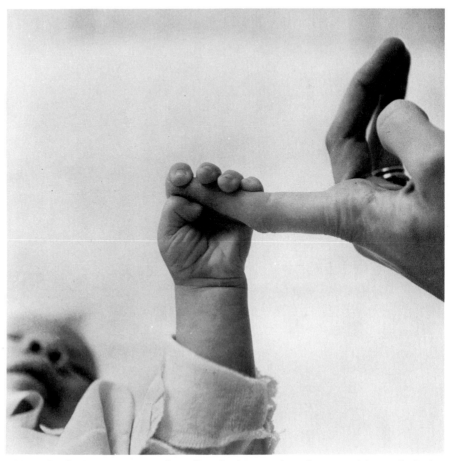

This individualistic grasp may be a throwback to a primate's grasp of its mother's fur.

later, Weismann proved his point. The offspring of the bobtailed mice were born with normal tails.

Later, an American writer named Albert Wiggam neatly skewered the Lamarckian fallacy as it applied to human beings. "If your father went crazy from a hit on the head with a brickbat," Wiggam said, "you do not inherit his cracked brain, but only his inability to dodge brickbats."

Animal research of a more sophisticated nature than Weismann's tail-bobbing experiments has yielded some intriguing genetic clues. Robert C. Tryon of the University of California, for example, has bred rat generations for more than a decade, seeking to find out if, by selective breeding, he could raise rats that could readily learn to scoot through the intricacies of a laboratory maze—or, on the other hand, could not. Tryon bred his rats exclusively to be "maze-bright" or "maze-dull," not for size, sleekness or other ratlike traits. When his generations of specialist rats became standardized, Tryon tested them in new mazes that the rats had never seen before. He found that the maze-bright rats were as adept as usual in the different mazes and the dull ones just as bumbling. In other words, maze-brightness was not a product of experience but a hereditary quality.

Tryon next sought to find if this quality was a single attribute or a combination. He set up experiments requiring both maze-bright and maze-dull groups to show discrimination in different tasks, such as judging distance and angles. The maze-bright rats did not display any marked superiority. This indicated that maze-brightness is a specific characteristic and not necessarily a mark of any general ability that might be considered all-round intelligence. The Tryon studies have continued, seeking to find measurable physical factors at the base of these hereditary bright and dull characteristics. This seemingly small issue is potentially significant. Somewhere in the body of the rat lurks the physical basis of maze-brightness or -dullness. If the biological bases for particular talents can be found in the rat, they may then be found in man.

Until the science of genetics makes this breakthrough (if it ever does), the reasons behind the inheritance of human talents and characteristics must be sought through observation. Simply tracing family histories suggests that artistic ability, for instance, seems to be inborn. The best example is the musical bent of the Bach family. Johann Sebastian, the great composer, belonged to one of seven generations of Bach musicians, including his father and four of his sons. So pervasive were the Bachs in German musical life that the family name came to be synonymous with musician, and to be the church organist in their home town was to be "the Bach."

Tracing genealogies may suggest links between individuality and inheritance, but more precise methods are needed for really convincing evidence. One such technique involves studies of twins, such as the sisters shown in the pictures on pages 26-37. Twins are a unique research source for unraveling the influence of heredity because there are two kinds: identical twins, who share exactly the same genetic background, and fraternal twins, who are genetically no more alike than ordinary brothers and sisters. By comparing a characteristic in identical twins with the same characteristic in fraternal twins, scientists can get a fairly clear idea of the extent to which heredity affects that characteristic.

In *The Psychology of Personality*, Jerry S. Wiggins and his associates at the University of Illinois reported striking results from a study of 20 pairs of twins during their first year. Nine sets were identical twins and 11 fraternal. The infants were tested each month for mental and motor abilities using a test called the Bayley scale, which scores manual dexterity in shaking rattles, reactions to stimuli like bells, responsiveness to adults shown by smiling or cooing, and so on. The authors reported: "Results of the experiment can be summarized in a single sentence; identical twins were more alike on every behavior dimension studied."

The same finding was recorded when the twins were studied for two universal phenomena—the social smile and fear of strangers. The raw, unlearned responses of identical twins were more alike than those of fra-

The social smile is the individual's first positive response to another person, a clear expression of pleasure at being part of human society. It develops when the infant can put the images of eyes, nose and mouth into the recognizable pattern of a face. The smile appears at the age of three to six months, depending partly on environment: a study found that babies in institutions smile at faces three weeks later than do those raised at home.

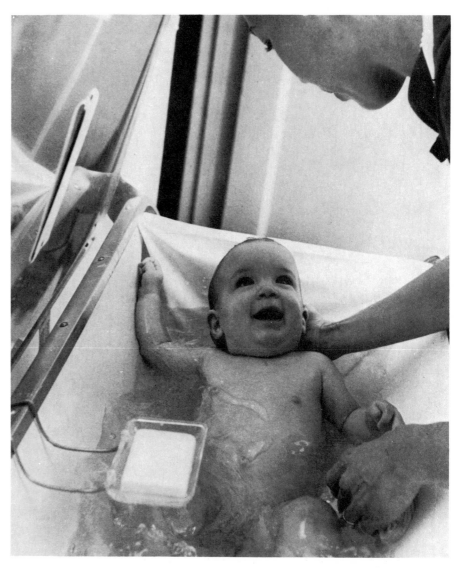

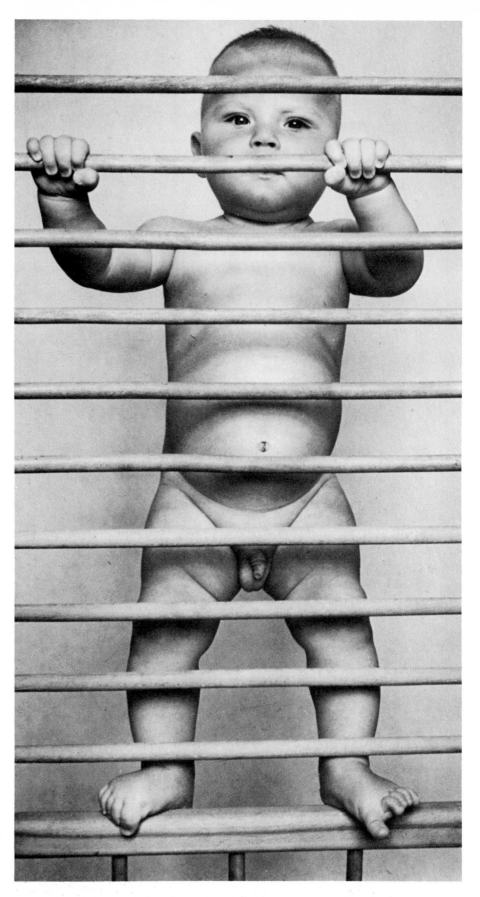

Climbing a ladder at the age of seven months, this diminutive gymnast demonstrates the value of training: from infancy he has been given a daily exercise period lasting 30 to 80 minutes.

A personal pace

A baby develops his own way of walking or crawling, on his own timetable. Some crawl until they are 18 months, others walk at nine months—and the seven-month-old at left climbs ladders.

The precocious climber is the protégé of a Czech doctor, Jaroslav Koch, who believes that the time it takes a baby to learn motor skills depends on the opportunity it has for exercise. Two weeks after this baby was born, Koch began urging him to raise his head; later he was taught to stretch for a toy. Practice in sitting, standing and crawling followed. Before the baby was eight months, he could swing from a trapeze.

Some babies like a one-knee-and-one-foot crawling style; this youngster prefers all fours.

Toes turned inward in a style that is distinctively her own, a sturdy 15-month-old walker circles around her mother (feet at right).

ternals. If identical twins show unmistakable evidence of inheriting certain characteristics, then presumably the behavior of all children is dictated at least in part by their genetic make-up.

One question, then, seems to be answered: children do inherit some of their individual characteristics—genetics plays a part in making them what they are. But this does not settle the question of the role of environment and the ways in which it interacts with heredity to determine the behavior of an individual. For from the doctor's first slap on the newborn's bottom, heredity runs head on (or tail first) into environment.

Heredity and environment are so closely and inextricably linked that it is impossible to isolate the precise effects of each in molding the individual. The problem has been posed succinctly by Donald Hebb, the Canadian psychologist: "Is it fifty per cent environment, fifty per cent heredity, or ninety to ten, or what are the proportions? This is exactly like asking how much of the area of a field is due to its length, how much to its width."

The interaction between heredity and environment shows up plainly in language. The human genetic constitution provides the physical equipment to produce speech. Further, it appears, the capacity to acquire language and use it correctly is also a genetic gift. Every human society, however primitive it may be in other respects, employs a language based on a complex set of rules that linguists call grammar. Every physically normal member of a society learns to use its language at an early age, absorbing the complex grammar without ever having been taught it explicitly. An English-speaking child naturally says "see the red ball" instead of "ball red see the." These facts have led linguists such as M.I.T.'s Noam Chomsky to conclude that the capacity to learn language is an innate part of man's biological equipment.

If Chomsky is right, this universal ability must cut across linguistic boundaries. The genes themselves speak no language; environment does. A Swedish child raised in Albania by foster parents will grow up speaking grammatically correct Albanian, not Swedish. There is a more extreme case: a baby who was the son of an English lord and who normally would have gone to Eton and Oxford and have acquired the distinctively accented speech of the British upper classes. But the child was born while his parents were on a secret mission to Africa. His mother and father died and he was stranded in the jungle. He was raised by a band of apes and grew up talking pseudo-ape: "Me Tarzan, you Jane."

In considering the environment of the emerging individual, it is necessary to step from the laboratory, where scientists analyze the heredity of mice and men, and enter the home. For it is in this small and rather private theater that the drama of a child's early development takes place. The principal actors, besides the child, are the mother and father, especially the mother, who in most cultures feeds the child, washes it, cuddles it and soothes away its infant griefs. The environment for the very young child is its home, its parents. How the parents act toward the child—the warmth, love, comfort and encouragement they lavish on their offspring, or fail to give it—determines in large measure how the child develops.

The most pervasive theory concerning the early childhood years and the effect of parental attitudes on the personality of the child was advanced by the pioneering psychologist Sigmund Freud *(pages 136-137)* around the turn of the century. It is difficult, in Western society at least, to conceive of the emergent individual without consciously or unconsciously reacting to Freud. He was the first influential psychological investigator to insist that the early years were decisive in the formation of character. And the influences he analyzed were ones that had previously been regarded as too indecorous or trivial to be accorded serious study: the pains and pleasures associated with eating, elimination and sex. (It is interesting to note that the scientist who shocked the world with his theories was himself a puritanical man who showed little interest in sexual activity and could not bear to explain the facts of life to his own sons.) While some of Freud's theories have been treated harshly by time, his bold assertion of the sexual nature of the very young and its effect on the psychosexual life of adults has revolutionized thinking about human behavior.

Freud believed that life instincts such as hunger and sex operate through a form of human energy called the libido. This energy is charged and discharged through sensitive erogenous zones like the mouth, anus and genitals. The infant's discovery and first use of its libidinous impulses occur in three stages—the oral, anal and phallic. Freud suggested that if a child passes through each stage successfully—that is, if it does not suffer from gross frustrations at one stage or another—then it will be more likely to have a fulfilled, integrated sense of self and be less likely to suffer from long-lasting psychic damage.

The first of these stages—the oral, or sucking, stage—involves the first libidinal pleasure. The mother's breast (or the substitute bottle) is the source of both life and joy. If a baby is deprived of this pleasure by too-early weaning, the result may be an enduring sense of deprivation and a lifelong urge to regress to infancy, where life's first source of satisfaction may be found and savored again.

The second of Freud's crises comes with the anal stage. Some time during the second year the infant learns to regulate consciously what has been automatic. The potty then can become the seat of pervasive emotional turmoil. Much, it seems, depends on the way the mother handles this stage of development. If, out of her own anal inhibitions—or if she is hooked on some prevailing theory of rigid toilet training—she tries too early to regulate the baby's natural release, the baby may retaliate. Feeling thwarted in this creative and satisfying activity, the little craftsman may hold back feces out of infant spite; in adult life, Freud's followers maintain, such a repressed individual may display behavior patterns of compulsiveness, stinginess and introversion. Or the infant may respond in quite the opposite way by soiling on purpose in order to distress the offending mother; it may even throw the feces, its handiest source of ammunition. Adults,

when angry, revert to a similarly infantile trick by hurling obscenities, and some experts believe that severe conflicts during the anal stage can give rise to cruel, vandalistic or sadistic tendencies.

The third and perhaps most controversial stage of Freud's infantile sexuality theory is the phallic stage. Freud held that by the end of the fifth year pleasure associated with the genital organs dominates the child's psyche. He believed that, while children of both sexes love their mother, their erotic fantasies fix on the parent of the opposite sex. If during this stage in the child's life there is some profound disappointment—the mother rejecting her son's love, for example, or the disappearance through divorce or death of the little girl's love object, her father—then there may be permanent damage to the child's sense of self and to its sexual identity. That much of the theory is not difficult. As Freud penetrated deeper into the sexual thicket, the trail becomes harder to follow. He discerned castration anxiety in the young male, a fear that the father will jealously deprive him of his penis to frustrate his sexual desire for the mother. At the same time, Freud said, the female child experiences penis envy. She thinks she is incomplete because she has only a cavity while the neighbor's child has a squirter, or whatever the going juvenile nomenclature calls it.

Not all psychoanalysts and psychologists agree completely with Freud. There are many hotly conflicting theories. Some of Freud's concepts today smack of male chauvinism. The famous psychoanalyst Karen Horney, who was trained in the Freudian discipline but later rejected his thinking about women, once remarked acidly: "I know just as many men with womb envy as women with penis envy." Horney felt that the emerging individual was not so much a mass of roiling infant passions as a tender, easily bruised but resilient creature that above all needed from its parents a sense of security. The seed of healthy self-realization lies in every individual, she believed, and will flourish if given half a chance.

Freud's analysis of infantile sexuality, greatly expanded and modified by later study, was seized upon as raw material for child-raising theories. Many conflicting fads have bewildered and even dangerously misled the well-intentioned mother. She has been besieged by both pro- and anti-breast-feeding partisans, advocates of no-nonsense toilet training and champions of the baby's right to set its own timetable, prophets of doom warning against permissive soothing of a crying baby and those who say such comfort is essential to the child's sense of security.

Fifty years ago, nearly all mothers breast-fed their babies. Then bottle feeding became a mark of enlightened motherhood in the Western world. The proper mother was the one who had enough sense to know that babies were usually inadequately nourished at the breast—and enough money to prepare formula. More recently, the bottle has been damned and breast feeding has been hailed, particularly among the middle and upper classes, as essential to normal development. A 1961 article in the *American Journal of Psychiatry* by the controversial anthropologist Ashley Montagu called breast feeding for at least nine months one of the "indispensably nec-

A mother's loving attention during childhood is crucial to the individual's development. As shown by this two-year-old seeking his mother's notice while she holds her eight-month-old baby, the need to share that attention can be traumatic. If the diminished attention given the older child is related to his being more grown up, his maturation may be aided. But if he feels rejected, he may grow up too unsure of himself ever to have satisfying relationships.

A timetable for social development

The individual's social development follows a definite schedule, but there are variations within the general pattern. Two-year-olds usually play with toys but not with one another; it takes another year before they will play together, even when seated side by side in the same room. Yet some six-to-eight-month-olds smilingly hug play partners.

The general but not invariable schedule holds through childhood. At three, most children learn to share their toys; yet some share at 18 months. At four, most children play almost exclusively in groups. But some are so fearful of others that they avoid groups until they are six or seven. Finally, at age five, most children display the rudiments of good citizenship, joining in cooperative play projects like building a house or managing a grocery. Not so that most individual child, the perennial loner, whose temperament has set him apart from birth. At almost any age, he resists all invitations to join the group, content within himself *(below)*.

At two, playing independently, a girl builds with some blocks while a boy tackles a book.

At four, youngsters willingly form a group for a nursery-school program—all but one, who shies away from his friendly neighbor's nudge.

At five, two Austrian boys and a girl are puppeteers and audience in a socially sophisticated form of cooperative play.

essary conditions for the well-being and healthy development of the infant. Any culture which discourages its mothers from behaving in this manner is likely to contribute in a major way to the predisposition to mental illness in its members." Predictably, this stern pronouncement was no sooner made than it was flatly contradicted. A study of 94 children by the University of California found that as long as the family atmosphere was congenial, there was no evidence "that breast feeding as such provides a psychologically better start for the child . . . than formula feeding."

But some of the twists in expert opinion that Freud inspired have been generally welcomed, if not universally endorsed. One of the most extreme of these changes in beliefs concerns masturbation. In the early part of this century, the prevailing view was propounded by Mary R. Melendy, a medical doctor and a Ph.D., who wrote a guidebook in which she advised mothers to teach a child that "when he handles or excites the sexual organs, all parts of the body suffer, because they are connected by nerves that run throughout the system, this is why it is called 'self-abuse.' The whole body is abused when this part of the body is handled or excited in any manner whatever. . . . The sin is terrible, and is, in fact, worse than lying or stealing! . . . It lays the foundation for consumption, paralysis and heart disease. It weakens the memory . . . it even makes many lose their minds; others, when grown, commit suicide."

Just how sharply the attitude toward masturbation has changed since Freud's ideas became current is reflected in a recent article in *Today's Health* by psychologist Wardell Pomeroy, one of the co-authors of the Kinsey Report, who said in part: "The major harm I see coming from the practice of masturbation is the guilt it generates. . . . Masturbation is an acceptable form of release. It is my hope that, in the future, the only questions about masturbation will be about how can it be used as a therapeutic tool and as an instrument of pleasure for both sexes."

At about the same time that Freud showed how sexual repression might affect individuality, a completely different line of research —studies of animals—began to reveal other influences. Experiments on dogs, rats, even pigeons proved that a calculated system of rewards could "condition" an animal to develop almost any desired ability, even one that would never appear naturally. Since then this "behaviorist" concept has been refined and expanded until some of its proponents, such as Harvard's B. F. Skinner, have come forward with prescriptions for influencing children to grow up into specific types of adults.

Skinner's idea, in brief, is that human beings can be scientifically programed from birth to be useful, nonviolent members of society. By a system of rewards the infant can be conditioned to behave well—to be gentle, cry little, learn quickly and so on. As the child grows it can be further conditioned by rewards to be cooperative, studious, well mannered. The adult result of this conditioning process, Skinner foresees, would create a model world free of war, pollution, crime, violence.

If Skinner's "behavioral engineering" smacks of 1984 in the nursery, the way he has put his theories into practice is not so forbidding. Skinner is the inventor of the air crib, designed in reaction to the "small jail" of the standard crib. The air crib has no barred sides, but is a roomy, air-conditioned and germfree infant container, glass enclosed. The baby needs only a diaper, thus is unconfined by clothing. It plays in complete safety, seeing out while others can see in. Skinner claims the crib provides more freedom for baby and mother, and does not curtail maternal affection since the mother can always slide open the door to give a bottle or a hug.

Skinner's emphasis on baby's need for motherly hugs is one point that not even his sternest critics will dispute. Of all environmental influences on the emerging individual, the critical one turns out to be simply love—affection, security, warm guidance. Its importance is one of those things everybody always knew. But how vitally important it is became clear only after repeated research on children who, for one reason or another, were deprived of love during their early years.

Several of these studies involved premature babies. As a rule such infants develop more slowly than full-term ones. It was long assumed that this occurred only because they were smaller, frailer and less developed to begin with. But the problem may be the special environment in which premies are kept. To guard against infection they are placed in incubators and deprived of normal maternal and nursely handling. Experiments show that handling such babies, even rocking their cribs, spurs weight gain.

But one of the most dramatic demonstrations of love's essential role was provided in 1945 by a classic study by the psychoanalyst René Spitz. In this study 239 children were observed, one group cared for by their mothers in an institution Spitz called the Nursery, the other group left to overworked personnel in the Foundlinghome, where one nurse had to look after 8 to 12 children. Thirty-seven per cent of the children in the Foundlinghome died during a two-year period, while not one was lost in the Nursery. Spitz reported that those who survived in the Foundlinghome were "emotionally starved," with severe problems in speech and walking, while the Nursery inhabitants were developing in healthy, normal fashion.

In normal families the touch of loving hands is something that both mothers and fathers are expected to provide, but because of the peculiarly intimate relationship of infant and mother, it becomes mainly a maternal function. Freud, who was the first of his mother's eight children and who was always favored by her, recognized the special advantage that a mother's love can confer upon a child. "I have found that men who know that they are preferred or favored by their mother give evidence in their lives of a peculiar self-reliance and an unshakeable optimism which often seem like heroic attributes and bring actual success to their possessors."

Freud, of course, was a special case. But his point is valid nonetheless. For it is the unique relationship between mother and child during the crucial emergent years that will largely determine whether the individual is to have a chance to realize its potential.

The Rational Animal

3

Of all the many qualities that distinguish one individual from another, none is more highly valued than intelligence. Call a person "stupid," and it is the ultimate insult, much worse than, say, "selfish" or "cheap." It hurts and infuriates the object of derision, and may guarantee the speaker a punch in the nose. On the other hand, compliment someone on his brightness and he may shrug deprecatingly but inside he glows with a warm feeling of pride.

The person with an extra measure of this basic human characteristic is prized because he is essential to his society, no matter what its form. People everywhere look to their wisest compatriots to solve the group problems, to make life run better and smoother; and in modern technological societies, particularly, there is a constant demand for the quick and the skilled to keep the machinery of civilization running. But superior intelligence is not so easy to identify as other individual advantages, such as beauty, physical strength or even magnetic personality. Intelligence blossoms slowly as a child matures, and may remain partly hidden in the "late bloomers" until well into adult life. The details of its nature remain difficult to analyze. Yet so great is the need for intellectual power that every human society—even those often called primitive—invents some kind of trial for sorting out its most intelligent members so that they can be developed into leaders. In advanced civilizations these procedures have been highly formalized for a very long period of time, and the existence of written tests intended to screen for intelligence can be traced back at least as far as 2,000 years.

The need to isolate intelligent individuals intensified with the Industrial Revolution, which demanded increasing numbers of people able to acquire increasingly complex training. Almost simultaneously the science of psychology was born, and it focused almost from the beginning on intelligence, trying to determine just what it is, how it can be defined, how it works and who has superior supplies of it. Psychologists developed new types of tests that, some of them hoped, would get at the most basic aspects of intelligence—identifying not only those who were smart but also those who had the capacity to become smart.

Whether these tests fulfill all the purposes expected of them has been a subject of worldwide debate ever since. The fiercest controversy has centered around the contention of some psychologists that the tests show the individuals of certain groups, races and even nations to be more intelligent than those of others. This argument goes beyond the nature-nurture controversy that clouds all analyses of human behavior, for it raises the question of genetic racial superiority and inferiority that today bedevils people throughout most of the world.

The heat of the argument over intelligence ratings is itself one measure of the value men place on this characteristic. It is a very human characteristic, mankind's distinguishing mark. All animals possess it in some degree, and people often draw on animal attributes to praise aspects of human intelligence. Expressions like "sly as a fox" or "wise as an owl" are frequently heard. But such comparisons do a man questionable honor, for at best an animal's slyness or wisdom is only a pale and blurry reflection of a human's.

There was a news story once about an elephant named Tuy Hoa, which learned to press lighted panels to win a sugar-cube reward. Eight years passed and Tuy Hoa did not see the panels. Then they were suddenly presented to it again, and 19 out of 20 times it pressed the correct ones. Congratulations to Tuy Hoa for never forgetting those panels. Congratulations also to the dolphin for being one of the brainiest of all nonhuman animals. When dolphins are not preoccupied with shooting basketball lay-ups in marinelands, they can be trained by navies to retrieve mines. Bright, brave dolphins.

But, however impressive animal achievements may seem, animal intelligence stops developing at a level ordained by nature while the human intelligence continues to progress. Chimpanzees, which are closest in form and function to humans, may master some human learning under laboratory conditions. They can even learn show business and, tricked out in costumes, perform on roller skates or grimace on cue. But the chimpanzees are not acting out their own concepts; they must be taught by man. The whale can sing piping ditties in its oceanic depths, but its massive life may be ended by a slender sand bar that strands it from its watery element. Man can plumb those same leviathan depths in submarines and rise to compose intricate symphonies on the land. The elephant can lift teak trees with its powerful trunk and ponderously tap numbers with its feet for circus audiences; man calculates the stress loads of cranes lifting steel beams that could break an elephant's back. The wise owl flies marvelously through moonless nights in order to locate and snare the minute mouse, but man creates radar to illumine his nights and to guide rockets to the moon. Man can make all of the elements his own by using a many-faceted, flexible intelligence that is alternately contemplative or creative, that can ponder the mystery of its own nature as easily as it builds a better mousetrap.

What is this mysterious but powerful tool, the human intelligence? There are almost as many definitions of the word as there are psychologists who have studied this elusive quality. Perhaps the best definition

"There go the most intelligent of all animals."

is one that was formulated, appropriately enough, by Alfred Binet, the great French psychologist who designed much-used tests to measure intelligence. Binet held that "the essential activities of intelligence" are "to judge well, to comprehend well, to reason well." This definition emphasizes the individual's ability to absorb information from parents, teachers, books, the environment—"to comprehend well." It also implies that the intelligent person is marked by the ability to make sense of this information—to "judge well" or "to reason well"—forming the facts into meaningful patterns that help the individual explain and deal with reality. These combined abilities to absorb evidence from the world and then perceive the interconnections between pieces of this evidence have enabled human beings to survive and to function effectively in an almost infinite variety of circumstances.

A definition such as Binet's applies equally to men in every culture; it characterizes the Micronesian islander who can navigate the trackless Pacific in his outrigger canoe just as aptly as it does the atomic physicist who comes up with new explanations for the behavior of the universe. The Micronesian navigator must learn to read sea and sky with meticulous accuracy in order to travel between pinpoints of land on an ocean featureless to the untrained eye. The scientist similarly comprehends observed facts about the universe that he then combines in logical ways to deduce physical laws. There are differences between the two problems, but the power to solve them both is the same—an observing, evaluating and combining process: intelligence.

Psychologists have long debated whether intelligence is a single general ability or is made up of a variety of components. A leader in the debate was the influential English psychologist Charles Spearman, who posited as early as 1904 a "universal Unity of the Intellectual Function." Spearman had noticed that people who scored well in vocabulary tests also tended to perform well in arithmetic and other examinations, while those who scored poorly usually did so across the board. This observation suggested that a general factor of intelligence, which Spearman called *g*, was present along with specific abilities, or *s*.

Taking a different tack, Louis L. Thurstone of the University of Chicago devoted much of his lifework to demonstrating that, while *g* may exist, it is more fruitful to view intelligence in terms of separable *s* components. Thurstone figured that there were at least seven components: memory, verbal fluency, verbal comprehension, skill with numbers, perceptual speed, spatial ability and inductive reasoning—and he developed special tests to measure the components. The concept that intelligence can be divided into separate components was picked up by J. P. Guilford of the University of Southern California, who proceeded to run away with it. He scrapped the *g* factor entirely and postulated no fewer than 120 special, separable mental abilities.

A different approach was later formulated by Raymond B. Cattell of the University of Illinois. Cattell suggested that intelligence is not compartmentalized or neatly divided into general and specific abilities, but rather is a continuum ranging gradually from native, or "fluid," intelligence at one end to acquired, or "crystallized," intelligence at the other. Cattell's fluid intelligence corresponds to the individual's genetic potential: it is the mind's raw, undeveloped ability. Crystallized intelligence is more akin to knowledge; it is what the brain has picked up and made sense of from the surrounding environment. In between the extremes of fluid and crystallized intelligence are subtle shadings of learned intelligence ranging from abstract reasoning through verbal and numerical skills to complex academic subject matter, such as literature, mathematics and science.

Many psychologists today, especially in the United States, lean toward Cattell's view, in part because it helps explain how heredity and environment cooperate to produce the individual's overall mental abilities. Some authorities, of course, are confirmed hereditarians, believing that intelligence is largely genetic in origin, while others are equally convinced that environment is the controlling factor. But most would probably agree that intelligence is the result of a subtle interplay of both genetics and environment. It is precisely this interplay—the intricate and frustratingly elusive relationship between fluid and crystallized intelligence—that makes the interpretation of intelligence tests such an extraordinarily complex process.

While all societies place a premium on intelligence, the demand for brain power is sharpest in the industrialized nations. They have large numbers of difficult tasks to perform, and to accomplish these objectives many intelligent people are needed. All highly developed societies employ a selection process designed to single out their most able citizens by measuring intelligence at some stage of the educational system. Most countries rely on examinations that determine academic achievement, testing students in their early teens on how much they have learned about basic school subjects such as mathematics, history and literature. Only those individuals who score high on these examinations are considered worthy of education for professional occupations; others are shunted into training for what are considered less-important positions. But many countries—particularly the United States—also use "IQ" tests, which attempt to gauge not learning, but rather aptitude for learning: the Stanford-Binet and Wechsler IQ tests, the U.S. Army's General Classification Test (the AGCT) and the College Entrance Examination Board Regular Scholastic Aptitude Test (SAT).

For half a century virtually every American school child had his ability examined with one IQ test or another, and in varying degrees the tests influenced his life. One man who attended New York City schools recalled how tests determined whether children were placed in "fast" or "slow" classes. "I remember that our classes were subnumbered 1, 2 and 3. Number 1 was considered smart, and 3 was average. But children assigned to 2 were publicly identified as dumb. It was a scarlet number and we children were not above using it cruelly. I suspect that 2 often became a self-fulfilling prophecy as both students and teachers in those classes were conditioned to expect poor performance and few worked to alter the test-certified inevitable."

Until recently, most American colleges rigidly governed admissions on the basis of the SATs, while in Europe the same control over a young individual's future was exerted by achievement tests. For servicemen, test scores determined who became a front-line infantryman and who a company clerk or a trainee in officers candidate school. Many businesses in many countries have used tests to screen applicants, and often the results have pigeonholed those employees who were hired. Intelligence tests, in short, have played a considerable role in determining who was well educated, who made how much money, what level of society individuals have reached, and, by extension, who their friends were and even whom they married.

All of these tests are predicated upon the same principle. They attempt to assess an individual's mental abilities by examining fragments of his intelligence. This, of course, is a basic weakness of testing. The problem confronting the testers is simply that human intelligence is too wide-ranging and complex to be measured directly. And so the tests focus on specific abilities such as verbal skills, spatial or mathematical abilities, or, in some cases, knowledge of certain subjects that may be remote from the immediate purpose of the examination.

Learning to tack his boat, a youthful Puluwat navigation student (second from right) is carefully supervised by an elder (right).

The islands' valued talent: navigation

Every society has its own standard of intelligence, geared to its needs for survival. Nations that are highly industrialized value individuals with scientific skills or organizational talents. Jungle-dwelling Brazilians pay homage to the teacher who can train young hunters by reciting from memory the details of every hunt in which he has ever taken part. Both men may be equally brainy; the uses to which they put their respective intelligences are determined by their very different cultures.

Among the people on the Pacific island of Puluwat, the job for which the brightest young men are trained is that of the navigator, for the atoll's survival depends on trade with other islands spread over 1,000 miles of ocean. To reach these islands, the Puluwatans use 40-foot outrigger canoes they hew out of local hardwoods, sailing them unerringly across open sea for 500 miles.

Training for this vocation begins at the age of 12. The apprentice makes hundreds of trips with a senior navigator to learn how the canoe handles under varying conditions. He is taught to detect underwater reefs by noting changes in the color of the water, to distinguish the various currents that affect speed between each island, to keep track of his position while drifting, to navigate in a storm and to recognize sea birds whose appearance can help point the direction in which he is headed.

Along with this training on the water, there are formal classes on land. The student must memorize a chart giving the rising and setting positions of 32 stars he will steer by at night. Then he must learn a map pattern that locates more than 50 islands relative to each other and to the stars. His learning is not considered complete until he can, at his teacher's request, start with any island in the ocean and rattle off the stars both going and returning between that island and all the others that can be reached from it.

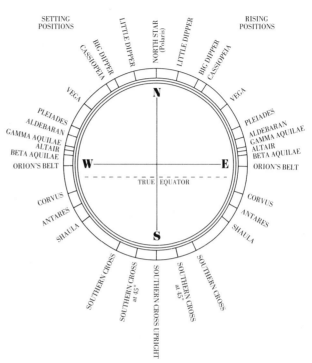

LITTLE DIPPER
BIG DIPPER
CASSIOPEIA
NORTH STAR (Polaris)
LITTLE DIPPER
BIG DIPPER
CASSIOPEIA
RISING POSITIONS
VEGA
VEGA
PLEIADES
ALDEBARAN
GAMMA AQUILAE
ALTAIR
BETA AQUILAE
ORION'S BELT
PLEIADES
ALDEBARAN
GAMMA AQUILAE
ALTAIR
BETA AQUILAE
ORION'S BELT

N

W   E

TRUE EQUATOR

S

CORVUS
ANTARES
SHAULA
CORVUS
ANTARES
SHAULA

SOUTHERN CROSS
SOUTHERN CROSS at 45°
SOUTHERN CROSS UPRIGHT
SOUTHERN CROSS at 45°
SOUTHERN CROSS

The star chart Puluwatans use resembles this Western version.

In a class session, the elder (far right) explains a navigation chart—pebbles arranged in a circle to represent the stars.

This approach is rooted deep in history. Intelligence tests, like so many modern contrivances, were first employed in ancient China. About 4,000 years ago it occurred to a Chinese emperor that it would be a sound idea to test his officials every three years and then promote or fire them according to how well they performed. The contents of the very first of these civil-service examinations are unknown, but Philip H. DuBois, a historian of mental testing, has reported that by 1115 B.C. the Chou Dynasty had standardized trials for the imperial bureaucracy. These examinations tested for proficiency not only in writing, arithmetic and music, but also in archery, horsemanship and knowledge of "the rites and ceremonies of public and private life."

Chinese written examinations, introduced about 200 B.C., changed over the centuries, taking their final form about 1370 A.D. By then a series of three competitive tests had been developed. Each examined the ability to handle a certain subject in the belief that performance in that limited area would predict ability (or lack of it) in a larger sphere. The first examination in the series, given each year in a city near the candidate's home, required the contestant to spend a day and a night in a booth composing a poem as well as prose essays on topics drawn from the writings of Confucius and other Chinese classics. If the candidate passed that test, he traveled to the provincial capital and spent three days and nights in solitude, writing away in both prose and verse. The few "promoted scholars" who survived that ordeal—at most 1 in 10—were invited to Peking for another round of examinations. The 2 per cent that passed this third test became mandarins and were eligible for high public office. The Chinese evidently assumed that if a candidate had mastered Confucian wisdom and could write about it eloquently, he would surely have enough ability for high-government employment.

Testing spread from China to the West in the 10th Century after medical examinations (which the Chinese had also invented) were instituted in Baghdad, the center of Islamic medicine, then the most advanced in the world. King Roger II of Sicily heard of the Baghdad examinations and decreed in 1140 that all the physicians of his island-realm be tested for proficiency. The ancient European university at Bologna began to give oral examinations in law in the 13th Century. Today's quiz-ridden school children can thank the teachers of the Jesuit order for making the first systematic use of written classroom tests in the 1500s.

Most of the early tests were designed to measure acquired knowledge, or crystallized intelligence, as Cattell would call it. Students were tested on their proficiency in particular subjects—medicine, Chinese literature or Roman Catholic theology. This system has an obvious defect. Good poets do not necessarily make good civil servants, so a poetry-writing test probably eliminates many of the best candidates for government jobs and passes some of the worst. Tests designed to ascertain just how much native intelligence an individual possesses, irrespective of school learning, did not originate until the first decade of the 20th Century. It is no accident

The quality of intelligence prized in Nigeria is the ability that enables this diviner both to memorize thousands of verses and to pick out those that are peculiarly appropriate for counseling his fellow tribesmen. The diviner begins studying verses as early as the age of six and must learn more than a thousand in order to qualify as a novice. When a tribesman comes for advice, the diviner shakes up the palm nuts (bowl at his left) and selects a suitable verse for recitation. Below is one for marital woes.

The god Ifa's wife Ore did not love him. When he went out in public Ore would insult him, and she had refused to cook for him. Angered, Ifa prepared a spell that would curse her with illness and loss of her cherished possessions. That very night, Ore had a bad dream; when she woke she went to a diviner. He said the dream was part of the punishment her husband had given her. Therefore she should wash his clothes, clean his house and make six loaves of pounded yams. When Ifa came home and saw what she had done, he removed the spell and welcomed his wife to his good graces.

that this type of test had its inception then. The burgeoning businesses created by the Industrial Revolution demanded increasing amounts of brain power and training. With this demand for talent came the need to know who was educable and to what degree—which people had the natural gifts to profit from education that would fit them for the tasks demanded by the new technological societies.

The brain-power requirements that arose in the 19th Century stimulated a rapid growth of educational systems. The big new schools were rather like factories, stuffing facts into pupils without regard to individual abilities; those who could not keep up were automatically rejected. Humane school officials became concerned for these rejected students and attempted to do something to help them. The pioneering English psychologist Sir Cyril Burt, for example, studied London children who were having difficulties in school to see whether they were simply slow in learning or were so lacking in native intelligence that they needed special schooling. It was with this same objective in mind that the French psychologist Alfred Binet set out to fashion his famous tool for gauging intelligence.

In the early 1890s Binet's own wide-ranging intellect—he was the author of successful plays as well as of scholarly tomes on hypnosis and the

The tests that rate intelligence

Intelligence and aptitude tests attempt to measure the individual's mental abilities in certain specific areas—verbal reasoning, numerical ability, space relations, abstract reasoning, mechanical reasoning and perception are the main categories. Typical questions from each category are reproduced below.

The tests shown here are designed not to determine how much a child has already learned in school, but to predict future accomplishment in higher grades or in college. They are used by teachers as an aid in understanding the individual student and in helping him plan a program of study. The questions shown were developed for youngsters of different ages, from kindergarten through the 12th grade. Answers are at the bottom of the opposite page.

Verbal Reasoning

1. Select from the lettered list the pair of words that best expresses a relationship similar to the one expressed in the following pair.

   CRUTCH: LOCOMOTION
   A. paddle: canoe
   B. hero: worship
   C. horse: carriage
   D. spectacles: vision
   E. statement: contention

2. One word has been left out of the sentence below. Choose the word that will make the best, the truest and the most sensible, complete sentence.

   Nature never rhymes her children, nor makes two men_____.
   A. alike B. hostile C. brothers D. different E. unique

3. If the words below were arranged to make the best sentence, with which letter would the first word of the sentence begin?

   by are fires carelessness many caused
   A. a B. b C. c D. f E. m

Numerical Ability

4. Subtract the times in the problem below and then select the correct answer from the lettered list.

   5 hrs. 13 min. 40 sec.
   3 hrs. 14 min. 50 sec.

   A. 1 hr. 58 min. 50 sec.
   B. 1 hr. 59 min. 50 sec.
   C. 2 hrs. 1 min. 10 sec.
   D. 8 hrs. 28 min. 30 sec.
   E. none of these

5. A party consisted of a man and his wife, their two sons with their wives, and four children in each son's family. How many were there in the party?

   A. 7 B. 8 C. 12 D. 13 E. 14

6. The tires of Carl's bike should each have 25 pounds of air, but he put 30 pounds in each. The amount of air he put in was what per cent more than he should have put in?

   A. 83⅓% B. 5% C. 120% D. 20% E. none of these

7. A man invested $800 and doubled his money at the end of each year. How much did he have at the end of four years?

   A. $4,000 B. $3,200 C. $12,800 D. $6,400 E. none of these

Abstract Reasoning

8. The four figures at left below make a series. Which of the five lettered figures would be the next, that is, the fifth one in the series?

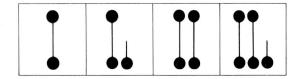
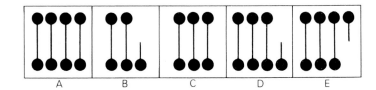

A B C D E

Mechanical Reasoning

9. Which chain by itself will not hold up the sign?

   A. Chain A   B. Chain B
   C. Chain C

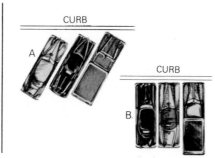

10. Which way can more cars be parked in one city street?

    A. Picture A   B. Picture B
    C. An equal number

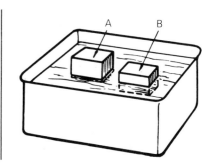

11. Which block weighs less?

    A. Block A   B. Block B
    C. Both blocks are equal

Space Relations

12. Which of the four boxes at the right below can be folded from the pattern at left below? The pattern shows the outside of the box.

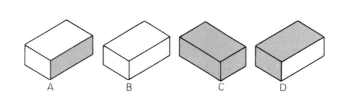

Perception

13. Which of the lettered pictures is exactly like the picture at left below?

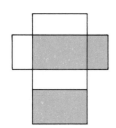

A

B

C

D

Answers: 1. D; 2. A; 3. E; 4. A; 5. E; 6. D; 7. C; 8. C; 9. B; 10. B; 11. A; 12. D; 13. D

Alfred Binet, inventor of the famous Binet intelligence test, first became interested in measuring processes of learning when he noticed that his daughters Madeleine (center) and Alice developed their skills at walking in different ways. Intrigued, Binet devised tests that showed they also thought differently—Madeleine was methodical and logical, Alice less so—and he then went on to create a basic plan for ranking an individual's intelligence according to the average for his age.

unconscious—became preoccupied with the mentality of children. He studied his own two daughters, Madeleine and Alice, writing a book on their intellectual functions, and also worked with children at a pioneering psychological laboratory housed in Paris' Sorbonne trying to measure their thinking processes.

By examining hundreds of school children, Binet and his co-worker Theophile Simon made what seems in retrospect to be an obvious discovery: children's intellectual performance improves with age. Binet observed, for example, that when children between 9 and 12 were asked to recall a sentence that had been read to them, their accuracy improved as their ages increased. If the ability to reproduce a sentence was one indication of intelligence (and Binet did not doubt that it was), then comparative performance at the same age with the same test material might reveal individual differences in ability. This discovery would be the keystone for all childhood IQ testing. (A similar idea had been conceived two decades earlier by an American doctor named S. E. Chaille, but his work attracted no attention and the luckless Chaille remains merely a footnote to the historic fame of Binet and Simon.)

In 1904, the Minister of Public Instruction in Paris asked a commission that included Binet to find a way to identify subnormal children in the public schools in order that they might receive remedial attention. Binet and Simon set about constructing more than 30 types of questions corresponding in difficulty with the varying abilities of children between 3 and 13. The tests ranged from rudimentary problems—imitate the gestures of the examiner as he rubs his head or points at his nose—to such sophisticated ones as the requirement to build a sentence around the words "forest," "carriage" and "snow." Binet and Simon tested groups of children of different ages to establish a standard for each age. Then if a nine-year-old suspected of being retarded could give satisfactory responses only up to the seven-year level, the suspicion of retardation was confirmed and the child was placed in a special class for what Binet called "mental orthopedics." Binet's tests worked well and he continually improved them, dropping items that experience showed did not clearly distinguish between age levels. He and Simon produced a definitive revision in 1911, just before Binet's untimely death at 54.

The Binet test is given by a trained examiner to one child at a time. The humane, child-loving Binet specified that the examiner was to take care that his approach to the child was "affected neither by . . . bad humor nor . . . bad digestion." Binet never assigned a numerical score to the results of his tests: the child was simply graded as normal, above normal or subnormal. Further, Binet warned against the "brutal pessimism" of those who believed test results were fixed for life. He recognized that children mature at different rates, changing—sometimes radically—as they grow and learn more of the world around them.

Binet's test became well established in France and other countries for its original purpose, to identify slow students who need special instruction. But in the United States it inspired the development of other, similar, tests intended to do something quite different: identify superior students. This type of test became the principal means of rating individual intelligence in America, largely because it promised to reveal intellectual potential wherever it might be—a goal suited to the egalitarian ideals of the country's educational system. As a result, intelligence testing became almost an obsession in the United States, with consequences that have spread far beyond its shores.

When the Binet-Simon test crossed the Atlantic Ocean it suffered something of a sea change. Along the way, a mathematical rating of the individual's test performance, devised by the German psychologist William Stern, was modified by the American psychologist Lewis Terman of Stanford University to give the original form of the well-known "intelligence quotient," or IQ = (Mental Age ÷ Chronological Age) × 100.

In this formula, chronological age is the actual age of the subject and mental age the age level reached on the examination. For example, if a six-year-old (chronological age) successfully completes items expected of a nine-year-old (mental age), then dividing 6 into 9 gives 1.5, which, when multiplied by 100, indicates a very superior IQ of 150. If the six-year-old completes six-year questions, 6 divided into 6 equals 1. Multiplied by 100 the result is, of course, 100, or normal. If, however, the six-year-old completes only the three-year level, then dividing 6 into 3 gives .5, which, when multiplied by 100, gives an IQ of 50—a level indicating mental retardation. Such numerical scoring is neat and efficient, but, despite later modifications, it suggests a precision that is illusory. The IQ figure is not an absolute measure, and an individual with a 200 IQ cannot be assumed to be twice as smart as one with a 100 IQ. But the seeming precision of the measure led teachers to take the IQ figures too seriously and, contrary to Binet's admonition against such "brutal pessimism," as final. Children were pigeonholed as "a 90" or "a 110," and were expected to perform at that mental level, too little allowance being made for the child's background, growth and educational efforts—in short, his individuality.

In spite of such drawbacks Binet's test, quantified into an IQ, received an enthusiastic welcome in the United States. Its first champion was Lewis Terman of Stanford, who substituted questions adapted to American children for some of Binet's French-oriented items and in 1916 published his revision of the Binet test. For more than four decades the Stanford-Binet IQ test was regarded as holy writ, the bible of U.S. intelligence measurement.

The Stanford-Binet was administered to one subject at a time, but later varieties of general-intelligence examinations were adapted to mass testing; they have been taken by generations of American school children, almost two million recruits in World War I, another nine million servicemen and -women in World War II, and no one knows how many job applicants, civil servants and corporate employees.

These various IQ tests virtually replaced examinations of learned knowledge as a means of screening able individuals for advancement in the United States; by the late 1930s achievement examinations in literature, history, mathematics and other subjects previously required for admission to American colleges and universities had been dropped in favor of the IQ type of intelligence test. A 1971 study, *College Admissions and the Psychology of Talent*, by Cliff W. Wing Jr. and Michael A. Wallach, both of Duke University, found that, although American college administrators insisted that they selected students for overall abilities, test scores remained the overwhelming consideration.

While the psychological intelligence test came to dominate the measurement of potential ability in the United States, it was not so widely used in other countries. They tested as vigorously as Americans, but continued to rely more on achievement tests.

The British had developed the famous, or infamous, examination called the eleven-plus (usually written 11+), which combined general intelligence questions with an academic-achievement section. The test got its name from the fact that it was given to most British school children some time around their 11th birthday.

The 11+ was a terrifying, make-or-break examination. The child who scored well on the test—and less than 20 per cent did—was eligible to go on to a state grammar school, which prepared students for university admission. University training in turn qualified the individual for high-pay, high-status employment in later life. But the child who scored poorly on the 11+ was usually consigned to a "secondary modern" school, which educated for the trades and pitched the youngster out into the labor force at the age of 15 or 16. The British phased out this horrific test in the 1960s, realizing that many children are slow starters and cannot reveal their potential as early as age 11, and replaced it with a series of achievement tests at later ages.

The French educational system—despite the fact that Binet was a Frenchman—never made general use of IQ tests. Instead, these tests have been used as Binet originally employed them—to identify subnormal children needing remedial schools. To gauge general ability, the French administer an academic-achievement test that terrifies as do few others. It is called the *baccalauréat* or, in French slang, the *bac*. This examination is taken at about age 18 by approximately 25 per cent of the student population graduating from the nation's academic high schools, or *lycées*. Only students who pass the examination are eligible to go on to the University of Paris (which includes the famous Sorbonne), the University of Grenoble or other great French seats of learning. The *bac* examines the students on all they have learned since entering school—mathematics, the entire range of the French literary classics, history and other subjects. The degree of fear the *bac* inspires is indicated by periodic attempts to steal the closely guarded test questions.

Western Germany, in contrast to England and France, has continued to use IQ-type tests widely and, in the manner of the old English 11+, relegates a vast majority of its students to technical and trade high schools, which they leave at age 15 to join the nation's work force. Less than 20 per cent of all German youths are sent to *Gymnasien*, the advanced high schools that lead to continued education at the university and ultimately to the better and usually more lucrative jobs.

In the Soviet Union, every school child takes a series of competitive examinations during the course of his school career. These tests are designed to sort out students in terms of the country's need for occupational specialists—nuclear physicists, tractor drivers, kindergarten teachers. They are purely achievement examinations; IQ tests are rejected by the Communist hierarchy on grounds that have been explained by A. A. Smirnov in *Soviet Psychology:* "If we reject the method of tests and measurements, does this mean that we do not think it is necessary to investigate the abilities of the pupils? No, we do not believe this. But we hold that a correct investigation of abilities is possible only if the child's activities are performed under his ordinary conditions of life, and when his abilities are not investigated statistically, but in their development and change, in connection with the whole personality of the child, his instructions and education, his entire life."

IQ tests are not anathema to the educational authorities of Italy, but they are not much used either. A few intelligence tests have been given in junior high schools on an experimental basis; otherwise Italy's schools put their faith in a series of academic-achievement examinations. Students are tested every spring on what they have learned during the school year. Then at the end of high school those wanting to go on to a university, a technical school or to other specialized studies must take one of the four tough academic-achievement examinations—called *esame di maturità*—set each year by the national ministry of education to test the candidates' fitness for their chosen fields.

The situation is much the same in Japan. Students are tested at each educational level for their mastery of mathematics, history, language and social studies. Teachers in primary and elementary school often do use IQ tests for their own guidance—to estimate the mental ability of the students they have to teach—but there is no official program for rating intelligence by IQ-type tests.

All of these tests, whether of the IQ type used so widely in America or the achievement type used elsewhere, work well in at least one respect: they identify young people who have the intelligence to master classroom tasks. Study after study has shown that those students making the higher scores on tests earn the higher grades in school. The IQ type of tests, in particular, may do the job too well.

Critics have charged, in effect, that colleges guarantee themselves student bodies that perform nicely only by admitting those with a proved talent for playing the education game. As humorist Peter de Vries put it: "Of course they graduate the best—it's all they'll take. . . . They will give you an education the way the banks will give you money—provided you can prove to their satisfaction that you don't need it." This may be a serious indictment of America's socioeconomic system or of the admissions policies of many of the nation's colleges, but it is also another way of saying that the tests are doing the job they are supposed to do: accurately predict academic performance.

Whether intelligence tests of any type also fill the broader role expected of them is another matter. They are relied on to detect intellectual ability, in order to select those people with the most potential for society. And it is true that the people the tests single out as bright generally achieve success in later life.

Terman demonstrated the value of his IQ tests in a long-term survey of the relationship between IQ and achievement. In 1922 he selected more than 1,500 children, most of them between the ages of 8 and 12, whose

The first mass test to determine individual differences in intelligence was the U.S. Army's Group Examination Alpha, here being given to World War I recruits in Virginia. Almost two million men attempted to answer its vocabulary, math and common-sense questions. The high score—207 out of a possible 212—was made by an ex-Yale professor.

IQs averaged a very superior 150. Terman, and after his death, his associates, followed this group from 1922 onward. And an elite group it proved to be. Only 11 out of 1,500 did not finish high school, and the number entering college was 40 times the national average. Later the group income proved to be twice the national average, and the 1,500 were top heavy with Ph.D.s and other earned academic honors.

If it is true that high scores on tests generally identify those with the intelligence to succeed in life, it is tempting to assume the converse: that low scores identify those lacking the intelligence to succeed. Indeed, this assumption has long been made. Now it is in doubt. The tests, by their very nature, may cause certain individuals to score low for reasons that have nothing to do with native intelligence.

All schemes for testing intelligence have come under increasing attack in recent decades on the grounds that they are unfair. They categorize people early in life, without taking account of varying rates of intellectual growth. It was concern over this drawback of testing that led the British to

A question of bias

One of the most vexing problems of intelligence testing is to formulate the questions so that they will measure a child's intelligence without regard to his background. The test items directly below illustrate the difficulty. The item on the right is sexually biased, since boys are more apt than girls to know how to carry heavy tools.

Those at left depend (1) on culture, requiring knowledge of the Louvre and the Bastille; (2) on residence, favoring country children over city ones; and (3) on wealth, involving familiarity with costly appliances.

No test is completely free of bias. But items like the one at bottom—which has deliberately cryptic instructions to avoid language bias—come as close as any that have so far been devised.

Culturally Biased Test Items

Each sentence has the first and last word left out. Pick the pair of words that will fill the blanks to make the sentence true and sensible.

1. ___ is to prison as Louvre is to ___.
   - A. warden—paramour
   - B. warden—museum
   - C. warden—France
   - D. Bastille—museum
   - E. crime—artist

2. ___ is to dog as Guernsey is to ___.
   - A. terrier—cow
   - B. bark—cow
   - C. tail—cow
   - D. tail—Jersey
   - E. bark—Jersey

Find the lettered pair of words that go together in the same way as the pair below.

3. HAND BEATER: ELECTRIC MIXER
   - A. broom: vacuum cleaner
   - B. flashlight: light bulb
   - C. mop: dish washer
   - D. wrench: vise

Sexually Biased Test Item

4. Which man finds the hammer easier to carry?
   - A. Picture A
   - B. Picture B
   - C. No difference

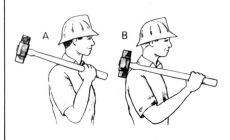

Culturally Unbiased Test Item

5. Fill the blank.

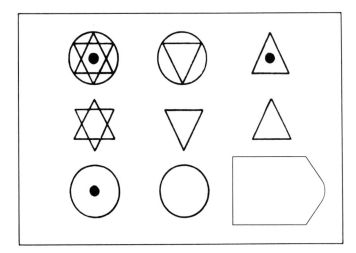

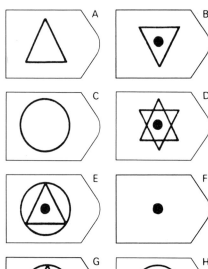

abandon the 11+. But an equally valid objection is the elitist nature of many tests. Achievement examinations, in particular, favor the privileged; those rich enough to attend the finest schools obviously can learn more of the knowledge being tested than a poor farm boy stuck in a rural educational system. The attempt to avoid this discrimination led to the American emphasis on IQ tests, which are intended to gauge not learning but intellectual ability, or fluid intelligence. Whether they actually achieve this goal is questionable.

The question of the IQ tests' fairness has assumed enormous importance because it bears on an issue that has kept the world in turmoil for centuries: ethnic superiority. In Asia, the Chinese and Japanese have been accused of lording it over their fellow Asians. In Africa, Indians and Levantines took over many of the key roles. On all continents until World War II, white Europeans ruled economically or politically or both. And since World War II, Europe itself has been torn by ethnic resentments, with Irish Catholics in Northern Ireland claiming they were downtrodden by Protestants and Spanish workers in France reporting discrimination. In many cases the dominant group—Chinese, British, white Americans or whatever—has justified its power over those it subjugated on the basis of an inherent superiority. Systematically, the subjugated were excluded from high government office, important business posts, social clubs and the better schools because they were considered, as a group, less intelligent and less qualified.

Racial superiority has been most sharply contested in America, and the results of intelligence tests have intensified the dispute. The IQ figures provided by the tests are undeniable. The scores of certain racial minorities —blacks, Puerto Ricans, Chicanos—almost invariably average lower than the averages of white Caucasians. If the tests are a fair measure of general intelligence, they would mean that intelligence depends on race, and is higher among whites than among others.

The genetic superiority of white people was assumed by some of the leading pioneer mental testers, whose writings reverberate with unabashed prejudice against humans of other skin colors. One early psychological investigator, Britain's Francis Galton, said: ". . . the number among the negroes of those whom we should call half-witted men is very large." Even Lewis Terman, the American adaptor of Binet's test, wrote of the Indian, Mexican-American and black children that he had examined: "Their dullness seems to be racial or at least inherent in the family stocks from which they come." Terman worked out the Stanford-Binet IQ scales by meticulously and laboriously testing his items on more than 2,300 children and adults. Significantly, Terman included only native-born white Americans in this test group.

More recently, Arthur R. Jensen of the University of California has been a leader among those arguing that some races are naturally inferior to others in intellect. Jensen has contended that while environment can be a factor in the lower IQ scores of ghetto-raised youths, heredity is far

Aptitudes and Occupations

Occupation	General Intelligence	Verbal Skill	Numerical Skill	Manual Dexterity
Medical Student	135	136	126	107
Computer Programmer	132	125	131	113
Dentist	132	121	124	111
Student Pharmacist	127	115	129	123
Accountant	118	115	121	*
Elementary-school Teacher	118	122	110	88
Air-traffic Controller	118	114	115	106
Social Caseworker	116	120	112	98
Machinery Salesman	113	109	107	98
Engineer	113	104	114	124
Patrolman	112	110	106	117
Bank Teller	111	110	110	101
Tool- and Diemaker	111	100	105	118
Clerk	108	109	111	*
Stenographer	108	104	106	103
Barber	101	94	99	120
Auto Mechanic	97	93	91	112
Asparagus Sorter	96	99	91	108

*not available

more important. Children from black and other racial minorities score poorly on IQ tests, Jensen has argued, not because the tests are intrinsically biased to favor America's white majority, but because minority-group children are simply not as good as whites at certain kinds of learning —their genetic potential is inferior.

Jensen's view has been attacked as racial bigotry by others who maintain that the tests (and the whole U.S. school system for that matter) are oriented to favor whites. Some of the more outspoken critics have declared that IQ tests are just another tactic employed by white people to rob blacks of the opportunity for good educations and general advancement in society. Even the milder critics have pointed out that since vocabulary plays a large part in many tests, white children from middle-class, culturally advantaged homes naturally have a decided edge over ghetto-raised blacks or children from Chicano or Puerto Rican homes, where Spanish is the first language.

Most psychologists argue that the questions on IQ tests inevitably reflect the culture of the persons making up the tests. To be fair, tests should examine the knowledge and reasoning ability that most children acquire at a certain age *within their particular society*. To take a simple example, Binet's early test required children to make change mentally in *sous*. Obviously, this problem would be useless in testing German children who count in *Pfennige*. Not so obvious are the class and cultural differences that exist within national boundaries. These differences are particularly acute in a culturally mixed country like the United States, where parts of the population have been isolated from the mainstream by racial, ethnic or economic circumstances. An amusing but pointed example was the case of a white Kentucky mountaineer child who was asked a question translated verbatim from the French Binet test.

"If you had taken ten cows to pasture for your father and six of them strayed away, how many would you have left to drive home?"

The impoverished youngster, who lived in the Appalachian hills where pastureland was so scanty that ten cows would be a herd—and a starving herd at that—replied: "We don't have ten cows. But if we did and I lost six, I wouldn't dare to go home."

A large body of more formal evidence indicates the influence of environment on the results of IQ tests. The United States Army Alpha test of World War I and the AGCT of World War II both showed that while whites from northern states tested higher than blacks from the same states, northern blacks performed better than southern whites. It seems that inferior southern educational environments had depressed both southern-white IQs and southern-black IQs.

Schools are only one element in the environmental influence on mental development. Social and economic factors play a major role. A study sponsored by the United States Department of Health, Education and Welfare shows a definite relationship between the scores of black *and* white children and the annual income earned by the family. Average scores in families earning less than $3,000 were far lower than those in the $7,000 to $10,000 bracket. At the top economic level, blacks and whites scored virtually even. All of the reasons for this are not completely understood. Harvard's Jerome S. Kagan, who argues that it is poverty and not race that helps to produce low IQs, believes that low-income mothers trying desperately to cope with myriad problems do not have the time or the energy to talk or play with their children and thus help them develop their intellectual potential. Since a disproportionate number of minority families are poor, this lack of maternal stimulation could account, in part, for lower scores from minority children.

Perhaps the most massive evidence suggesting that racial minorities are not genetically inferior in intelligence has been the exhaustive 1966 Coleman Report on American education. James S. Coleman, a sociologist at Johns Hopkins University, led a team of researchers that studied more than 600,000 children in 4,000 schools. The report showed minority children lagging behind whites at every elementary-grade level. But one of the study's conclusions was that black children enrolled in schools where middle-class whites are in the majority perform better than black children in predominately black schools. In other words, children do better when a school atmosphere favors educational aspiration, and where academic performance is relatively high. It does not matter, the Coleman Report continued, whether the schools themselves are new or antiquated, well or poorly equipped; the school atmosphere is what counts. If there is an at-

mosphere of positive educational achievement, the minority children rise well above the performance level attained by similar children in ghetto schools. Many black educators are quick to point out that such an atmosphere of positive educational achievement can be created whether the student body is mixed black and white, all white or all black.

In recent years criticism of intelligence tests has caused them to be abandoned in many places and situations. Industry in the United States no longer uses general IQ-type intelligence tests to examine the abilities of job applicants. The United States Supreme Court outlawed this practice in a 1971 decision in a case called *Griggs* v. *The Duke Power Company*. Willie S. Griggs was employed as a laborer by the North Carolina utility and was denied a better job after doing poorly on an IQ test. He brought suit, claiming that the company was violating his civil rights. The Supreme Court supported Griggs, saying that it was proper to give an applicant a test related to a specific job—for example, somebody applying for work as a typist could be tried with a typing test—but that general-intelligence examinations could not be used as job-qualifying tests.

A parallel development has occurred in some school systems. As a result of criticism of intelligence tests, schools in New York City,

Washington, D.C., and Los Angeles abandoned IQ-type examinations in the lower grades (they employ reading tests instead).

Intelligence tests need not be discarded, however, to eliminate discrimination against individuals. Used properly, their apparent bias can be canceled out. One approach has been pioneered by Wesleyan University in Connecticut, which selectively lowered test requirements for entering students. In 1965 Wesleyan admitted 32 blacks from poor educational systems with verbal SAT scores averaging 116 points below the median for all of the university's students. But each of the blacks was bright by comparison with his high school classmates, explained Wesleyan Admissions Dean John Hoy after the experiment had been underway for four years. "In many ways he was already a man. He had the drive he needed to get as far as he did in a poor educational system. So far—knock wood—our black academic attrition is about the same as white." Dean Hoy, in other words, was assuming that intelligence is equally distributed between blacks and whites and that it is merely the blacks' environment that causes the blacks' SAT scores to be lower than those of whites. Hoy left Wesleyan in 1969, but the succeeding administration has continued the experiment successfully, relying on the SATs to pick out the most gifted students from within each segment of the population.

The Wesleyan experience seems to confirm the belief that tests give a useful comparison of intelligence among individuals with similar social and economic backgrounds, but are inadequate for comparing intelligence across cultural and class boundaries. If there is no way to compare intelligence between cultures, there can be no valid evidence that any racial group is superior or inferior to any other in intelligence. And in the absence of such evidence, most scientists take the view that native, or fluid, intelligence is, like other human characteristics, uniformly distributed among all races and ethnic groups of the world.

The Biblical parable of the good seed falling on barren ground seems to apply to individual intelligence. It too can grow and flourish if nurtured, as Alfred Binet recognized almost a century ago. For each person, any measurement of how much intelligence he allegedly has should be far less important than what he does with it.

The Creative Urge

4

"In the beginning God created the heaven and the earth." This reported divine act of creation may have set an example in creativity for the mortals who inherited His earth. Certainly, the creative urge is the most profoundly human—and mysterious—of all individual attributes. Animals have considerable intelligence and they display distinctive personalities, but among them creativity is essentially nonexistent. Aside from such questionable examples as a rare bird that decorates its nest with bright pebbles and flower petals, man is earth's only creator. He has been at it ever since the species evolved; taming fire is a creative development of a high order.

Man's creative efforts have ranged from the sublime, like Michelangelo's Sistine ceiling depicting God's own creation, to the ridiculous, such as the advertisement in a recent newspaper urging consumers to visit a certain shopping center for a "creative shopping experience." In between, there has been a staggering quantity of marvelously varied individual creation spread among all the world's cultures, sometimes mysteriously flaring up like novae in a certain place and time to dazzle all who behold it. Mexico's Maya, the Benin of Africa, Athenians of the Periclean Age, the Ming Dynasty of China and Italians of the Renaissance are only a few examples of cultures in which creativity flowered abundantly during certain epochs, and then dropped off like a spent flower when whatever psychic energy had fueled its growth was used up.

But beyond the productions of masterworks in art and science, ordinary individuals too may be creative. The chef or housewife whipping up a recipe never before attempted, a fisherman tying a fly that no trout in history has previously been tempted with, all are engaged in a form of creativity. Dalton Trumbo, in his war novel *Johnny Got His Gun*, has a bittersweet moment when the cruelly wounded soldier recalls that his father "raised sweet corn and summer squash and cantaloupes and watermelons and cucumbers. He had a great hedge of sunflowers around it. . . . His father would get up at five or five thirty in the mornings to go out and irrigate the garden. He would come home from work in the evenings eager to return to it. The garden in a way was his father's escape from bills and success stories and the job at the store. It was his father's way of creating something. It was his father's way of being an artist."

If such homely examples are included in a definition of creativity (and there seems to be no reason to avoid them), then creativity is not just the isolated work of genius but a fertile continuum of human life into which seeds from all may fall and sprout.

Certain individuals, too, have been blessed with a richness of creative power that sets them above all other people. William Shakespeare turned out an average of two plays a year during his writing life—36 dramas in all—many of which deserve to be numbered among the greatest literary works of all time. Leonardo da Vinci was a human volcano of ideas and works, spewing out a creative torrent ranging from the *Mona Lisa* to sketches of armored tanks and flying machines.

Creativity is not necessarily linked to artistic talent. Ordinary individuals on any given day may satisfy the dictionary definition of the verb create: to bring into being; cause to exist. The concept involves a fresh way of seeing and making sense of anything. Part of creativity is heightened perception, an ability to recognize significant aspects of the world that others might miss. Another part is an ability to make connections, to relate observations in a meaningful way. And a third part is the courage and drive to make use of the perceived interrelations, to apply them to achieve some new result. These facets of creativity are involved in all the great works of genius, but so are they involved in homelier activities.

For the standard dictionary definition has been expanded by some modern psychologists. The extent to which they are willing to go is exemplified by Abraham Maslow of Brandeis University, who tells of a woman, "uneducated, poor, a full-time housewife and mother," who did none of the conventionally creative things "and yet was a marvelous cook, mother, wife and homemaker. With little money, her home was somehow always beautiful. She was a perfect hostess. Her meals were banquets. Her taste was impeccable. She was in all these areas original, novel, ingenious, unexpected, inventive. I just *had* to call her creative." As Maslow sees it, the essence of creativity resides in qualities—the "original, novel, ingenious, unexpected, inventive"—that may appear in anyone.

Others go even further than Maslow. Claims of creativity have been made on behalf of advertising people who compose songs about armpit sprays, politicians adept at swaying multitudes, generals and statesmen rearranging maps and boundaries.

The reverence in which the processes of creativity are held and the lengths to which people go in claiming that their work is creative have been satirized by the humorist S. J. Perelman. "I had my own business up in Hollywood," a character in a Perelman story says, "a few doors from Grauman's Egyptian, on the Boulevard. We eternalized baby shoes—you know, dipped them in bronze for ashtrays and souvenirs. The work was creative, but somehow I felt I wasn't realizing my potentialities."

Few would insist that bronzed baby shoes are the work of creativity. The creative process involves both skill and imagination, and it requires an inventiveness and originality that go far beyond the "eternalizing" of baby's shoes. One way to track the creative process is to examine how famous scientific breakthroughs occurred—what the steps were that led to bursts of original thinking. Another is to see how highly creative people have explained their own methods. A third way to examine the creative process is to analyze the environments that seem to nourish creativity, and assess tests that attempt to identify creativity's components and their relationship to intelligence. This chapter will explore all of these avenues in an effort to identify this quicksilver quality, explain how it works and show how it may be encouraged.

One form creativity seems to take is the sudden flash of insight, an idea that pops into the head—as the cartoonist depicts it, a light bulb suddenly going on, pow! This is what Arthur Koestler, himself a very creative novelist and critic, calls the Eureka process, illustrated by the story of the ancient Greek scientist Archimedes leaping naked from his tub shouting "Eureka!" (I have found it!).

What Archimedes had found was the way to measure whether the gold in the crown of King Hiero II, tyrant of Syracuse, was pure. Archimedes' inspiration supposedly came from the water spilling over the edge of a full tub when he stepped in; he realized that the volume of overflow exactly equaled the volume of his leg, suggesting an easy way to measure the volume of anything, even an intricately ornamented crown. He also knew that the crown would be heavier if made of pure gold than if alloyed with silver (gold is denser than silver); consequently, if an alloy crown were to be the same weight as a gold one, its volume would have to be greater. So Archimedes compared the volume of the crown with the volumes of an equal weight of gold and of silver, immersing each separately in a filled container of water and gauging the overflow. The crown displaced exactly as much water as the gold, but less than the silver, and Archimedes could reassure Hiero that he wore the real thing.

The significance of Archimedes' discovery goes far beyond the mere solving of the problem of weighing the King's crown. His act was creative because he was the first to perceive a fundamental principle of physics, the principle of buoyancy, which holds that a body immersed in a fluid loses as much weight as the weight of the fluid it displaces. This basic law has come to be known as Archimedes' principle, in honor of the creative genius who was first to grasp it.

Archimedes' solution may seem obvious in retrospect, but it only became obvious in the mind of Archimedes, who was capable of performing what Koestler calls bisociative thinking. This forbidding phrase means the ability to think on two planes simultaneously. The mind is at once able to make connections between two dissimilar ideas or objects or contexts to create a harmony between them, a spark leaping between the conscious and the subconscious, as it were.

Not all creative discoveries come upon their discoverers like a flash of light, however. In fact, the inventor of the light bulb, ironically perhaps, took another, longer, more laborious route. Thomas Edison was the man

Yielding to the urge for self-expression, a school child scrawls her name and an original flourish of flowers on the pavement of a city street.

A graduate student expresses his special interest in the culture of the Eskimos by carving a wooden paddle with primitive implements.

Arms upraised in feigned ferocity, an African Bushman gives vent to his acting ability by dramatizing folk tales for fellow villagers.

Self-expression: spark for creativity

The creative impulse in every human springs from a need for self-expression. The urge is universal—everyone has sought at one time or another to translate his innermost thoughts and feelings into visible outward form. A small child's ripening ego may prompt her to chalk her name on a city street. People all over the world express themselves in such familiar ways as singing, dancing, sculpturing and storytelling.

Every act of self-expression stands on the brink of creative achievement. Seasoned with talent, inventiveness and originality, even a mundane product can be invested with freshness and value. "A first-rate soup," psychologist A. H. Maslow has observed, "is more creative than a second-rate painting."

A puppeteer expresses himself through the medium of a papier-mâché Punch and Judy.

who, by placing an incandescent filament in a glass bulb, lit up the world. Yet the principle of the incandescent filament was not invented by Edison. His achievement was preceded by a long line of similar filaments that had not worked successfully for *their* inventors; he himself tried hundreds of metallic combinations in his laboratory before hitting on the right one. Edison's ability to create something new and valuable owed much to his energy and tenacity, as befitted his own definition of genius: 1 per cent inspiration, 99 per cent perspiration.

Yet the creative processes of Edison and Archimedes had much in common and followed the same rough progression. First there was what might be called the intake stage: both saw the problem that the world presented to be solved and were aware of previous steps taken toward that goal. Then there was an incubation period when their minds consciously or unconsciously worked toward a solution. The biologist Paul Saltman has described his own use of this part of the process: "I'm sort of like a ruminating cow. I'll pick data up, chew on it for a while, swallow it, pop it up again, and chew on it a little more." The third part of the process could be called revelation—dramatically sudden in Archimedes' case—of the solution, the creative idea.

Further insights into the nature of creativity can be gained from accounts that creative people in the arts and sciences have written of their own inventive processes. Among them are the French mathematician Henri Poincaré and the English poet A. E. Housman. Poincaré tells how he wrestled with mathematical problems called Fuchsian functions, which happily do not have to be understood in order to follow his process:

"For fifteen days," wrote Poincaré of the intake stage, "I strove to prove that there could not be any functions like those I have since called Fuchsian functions. I was then very ignorant; every day I seated myself at my work table, stayed an hour or two, tried a great number of combinations and reached no results." The incubation period was set off, as it has been for many others, by drinking something. "One evening, contrary to my custom, I drank black coffee and could not sleep. Ideas rose in crowds; I felt them collide until pairs interlocked, so to speak, making a stable combination. By the next morning I had established the existence of a class of Fuchsian functions. . . . I had only to write out the results, which took but a few hours."

Poincaré wished to delve deeper, but a geology trip intervened and he put aside the mathematics, awaiting the revelation. "Having reached Coutances," he wrote, "we entered an omnibus to go some place or other. At the moment when I put my foot on the step the idea came to me, without anything in my former thoughts seeming to have paved the way for it. . . . I went on with a conversation already commenced, but I felt a perfect certainty. On my return to Caen, for conscience' sake, I verified the result at my leisure."

Poincaré then repeated some steps of the process, since still further theoretical territories remained to be taken. "I made a systematic attack upon them and carried all the outworks, one after another. There was one however that still held out, whose fall would involve that of the whole place . . . . Thereupon I left for Mont-Valérien, where I was to go through my military service; so I was very differently occupied. One day, going along the street, the solution of the difficulty which had stopped me suddenly appeared to me. . . . I had all the elements and had only to arrange them and put them together. So I wrote out my final memoir at a single stroke and without difficulty."

The poet Housman went through a process with words and rhythms similar to the one Poincaré used on numbers and mathematical symbols, but beer, not coffee, oiled his creative machinery. He wrote:

"Having drunk a pint of beer at luncheon—beer is a sedative to the brain, and my afternoons are the least intellectual portion of my life—I would go out for a walk of two or three hours. As I went along, thinking of nothing in particular, only looking at things around me and following the progress of the seasons, there would flow into my mind, with sudden and unaccountable emotion, sometimes a line or two of verse, sometimes a whole stanza at once, accompanied, not preceded, by a vague notion of the poem which they were destined to form part of. Then there would usually be a lull of an hour or so, then perhaps the spring would bubble up again. I say bubble up, because, so far as I could make out, the source of the suggestions thus proferred to the brain was . . . the pit of the stomach."

The course of creation did not always run smooth. Housman told of one four-stanza poem: "Two of the stanzas . . . came into my head, just as they are printed, while I was crossing the corner of Hampstead Heath between the Spaniard's Inn and the footpath to Temple Fortune. A third stanza came with a little coaxing after tea." But the fourth and final stanza was a different cup of tea altogether. It took him, Housman said, one year and 13 rewrites to capture it.

Housman's poetic predecessor Samuel Taylor Coleridge had a far stranger tale to tell about the creation of one of his famous poems, "Kubla Khan." If we are to believe Coleridge, poetry can come like the cartoonist's light bulb. Or to use a more appropriate lyrical simile, like winds of celestial inspiration streaming in to fill a void in the poet's soul. "Kubla Khan," with its opening lines of unearthly beauty,

In Xanadu did Kubla Khan
A stately pleasure-dome decree:
Where Alph, the sacred river, ran
Through caverns measureless to man
Down to a sunless sea,

is subtitled "A Vision in a Dream." And that, Coleridge claimed, is exactly what it was. He reported that one night after taking a medicine called laudanum, which contained opium, he read a sentence in *Purchas his Pilgrimage*, a 17th Century travel book, that said: "Here the Khan Kubla com-

Unlikely creators

Some of the most extraordinary creative achievements have been made by the most unlikely creators. Laborers have become philosophers, and mathematicians, authors. The French primitive painter Henri Rousseau was also a customs official; two Americans, poet Wallace Stevens and composer Charles Ives, were insurance executives.

Perhaps the most unusual creator pictured here was a fish peddler named Bartolomeo Vanzetti. He and Nicola Sacco, a shoemaker, were sentenced to die in the electric chair for murdering a paymaster and a guard during a 1920 holdup in South Braintree, Massachusetts. Many people think they were wrongly convicted for political reasons —the two were immigrants and anarchists at a time of anti-immigrant, antiradical fervor. They died insisting they were innocent, but not before Vanzetti had created the eloquent statement reprinted on the opposite page.

Eric Hoffer

Although he had no formal education, Eric Hoffer used his experience as a migrant farm worker, gold prospector and longshoreman to write books that earned him a reputation as America's philosopher of the workingman. Since 1951, his eloquent and original reflections on the nature of man and society have been translated into a dozen languages.

Grandma Moses

Anna Mary Robertson Moses did not begin to paint in earnest until she was in her seventies. For the next quarter of a century, until she died at the age of 101, Grandma Moses drew on her memories of life as a farm child, hired girl and farmer's wife to paint what she called old-timy landscapes. Her primitive style impressed the critics and delighted the public; some of her paintings were sold for as much as $10,000 apiece.

Simon Rodia

Tile-setter Simon Rodia (left) labored 33 years on a monument in Los Angeles. One critic called the work, known as the Watts Towers, "a masterpiece of primitive sculpture."

Sacco and Vanzetti

Convicted of murder, Nicola Sacco (right) and Bartolomeo Vanzetti (mustache) were sentenced to death. Vanzetti's grammar was flawed, but he wrote a powerful statement.

"If it had not been for this thing, I might have live out my life, talking at street corners to scorning men. I might have die, unmarked, unknown, a failure. Now we are not a failure.... Never in our full life can we hope to do such work for tolerance, for justice, for man's understanding of man, as now we do by an accident.

Our words—our lives—our pains—nothing. The taking of our lives—lives of a good shoemaker and a poor fish peddler—all. That last moment belong to us—that agony is our triumph."

Lewis Carroll

As Charles Lutwidge Dodgson, he was a fine amateur photographer as well as a professional mathematician. Then, in his thirties, using the pen name Lewis Carroll, he startled British literary circles by writing two of the world's most imaginative children's books: "Alice's Adventures in Wonderland" and the sequel, "Through the Looking Glass."

The Wright Brothers

Starting out as bicycle builders, the brothers Orville and Wilbur Wright used their knowledge of mechanics to solve the riddle of flight. In 1903, after years of experiments with models, they revolutionized transportation with a 12-second flight in the "Kitty Hawk," their first powered machine.

manded a palace to be built and a stately garden thereunto." Immediately he fell asleep, said the poet, and in his sleep composed no less than two to three hundred lines of the poem without any sense of strain or effort.

"On awakening," wrote Coleridge, referring to himself in the third person, "he appeared to himself to have a distinct recollection of the whole, and taking his pen, ink, and paper, instantly and eagerly wrote down the lines that are here preserved. At this moment, he was unfortunately called out by a person on business from Porlock, and detained by him above an hour, and on his return to his room, found, to his no small surprise and mortification, that though he still retained some vague and dim recollection of the general purport of the vision, yet, with the exception of some eight or ten scattered lines and images, all the rest had passed away like the images on the surface of a stream into which a stone has been cast."

Some experts say that this explanation demonstrates Coleridge's vivid imagination at its best, constructing an alibi for the fact that his creative fires failed, leaving "Kubla Khan" a fragment of only 54 lines. But Coleridge did take laudanum for a variety of illnesses and the man from Porlock (to lovers of Coleridge's poetry the most detested interrupter in English literary history) seems too real to have been invented. In any case, a number of poets besides Coleridge and Housman have attested that poetry has just come unbidden, words somehow combined by their unconscious minds to reveal new ways to order the old relationships of people and things. Most have also confessed, however, that their creations, like Edison's, have cost them a great deal of perspiration. The apparent dif-

Uninhibited responsiveness, manifested here by a Japanese boy reacting to a snowfall, is characteristic of children the world over, but is rarely experienced by adults. When it is, this intensity of feeling can lead to works of great creativity.

ferences, however, are details. Whether inspiration arises from beer, coffee, a dream or sheer hard work, the three stages of the creative process seem to be general, identifiable in almost all cases.

While creativity seems to be a universal quality, put to use by a more-or-less-general method, it is by no means uniformly possessed or applied by all human beings. Many efforts have been made to analyze why and how it flowers, and they have led to some surprising insights. A few psychologists even believe they can tell what sorts of people, from what kinds of families, are likely to be highly creative—and when.

For one thing, creativity is the specialty of the young. Many experts have noticed that the gifted—of any age - retain a childlike inquisitiveness and receptivity. But more striking is the early age at which most creative achievements take place.

In an exhaustive study of creative accomplishers entitled *Age and Achievement*, H. C. Lehman scrutinized the lives of thousands of outstanding men and women over the centuries and found that creativity generally shows itself early in life, though it may continue for many years. One of the subjects Lehman surveyed, Justice Oliver Wendell Holmes Jr., summed up the age-creativity relationship bluntly: "If you haven't cut your name on the door of fame by the time you've reached 40, you might just as well put up your jackknife." Holmes's father, as a matter of fact, had achieved fame at 21 with his enormously popular poem, "Old Ironsides," which saved the U.S. frigate *Constitution* from being scrapped.

Lehman showed that early achievement applies both to the sciences and to the arts. Original contributions to chemistry are generally made by people between 26 and 30, in mathematics between 30 and 34, in medicine between 35 and 39. The arts are also the province of the young, the peak years for great lyric poetry being the ages of 22 to 26, for symphonies 30 to 34. (Novelists and architects are exceptions; they seem to do their most innovative work at the hoary ages of 40 to 44.) The accomplishments of certain prodigies are astonishing: Lehman notes that the English poet John Keats wrote his odes and dozens of other superb poems between the age of 20 and his early death at 25; Alexander Pope began writing publishable poetry at 17; the British statesman of the 18th Century, William Pitt the Younger, was Prime Minister at 24; Mendelssohn composed his overture to *A Midsummer Night's Dream* at 17; Mozart wrote hundreds of great works before his death at 35.

Even more surprising than creativity's connection with youth is its relationship to superior intelligence. There does not seem to be any. Many highly intelligent people are not at all creative, and many highly creative people are not especially bright. Evidence that the smart may not be creative is provided by the long-range study of unusually intelligent Californians conducted by Lewis Terman, the originator of the Stanford-Binet IQ test, and his co-workers at Stanford University. Almost all of these high-IQ people did very well in life; not one of them produced any outstanding creative works.

Finding beauty in the prosaic

Creative individuals look at the same things everyone else does, but they do not always see the same things. They are endowed with a heightened perception, and they get beyond the obvious to discern nuances of shape, texture and light that reveal unsuspected patterns in the most familiar objects.

This fresh way of looking at things is eloquently demonstrated in the work of three photographers—Aaron Siskind *(left)*, Edward Weston *(center)* and William Garnett *(right)*. Each of these artists has taken a subject that most people would have overlooked and, by applying his extraordinary perception, transformed it into something of great beauty. As Edward Weston described this process: "Guided by the photographer's selective understanding, the penetrating power of the camera-eye can be used to produce a heightened sense of reality—a kind of super-realism that reveals the vital essences of things."

Paint chips clinging to the wall of an abandoned hospital become abstract art in this photograph by Aaron Siskind. "The object is often unrecognizable," Siskind says in explaining his technique. "It has been removed from its neighbors and forced into new relationships."

What Edward Weston perceived in a leaf
of common cabbage made this famous
photograph. In his diary he wrote of it:
"Cabbage has renewed my interest,
marvelous hearts, like carved ivory, leaves
with veins like flame, with forms
curved like the most exquisite shell."

In order to capture on film the changing
patterns of landscapes, photographer
William Garnett learned to fly a plane,
often spending days searching for the
right angle and light. These sensuously
curving shapes are sand dunes in Death
Valley, seen from his special vantage.

This observation was verified by Donald MacKinnon of the University of California, who focused mainly on architects. "Architecture," MacKinnon explains, "as a field of creative endeavor requires that the successful practitioner be both artist and scientist. . . . The successful and effective architect must, with the skill of a juggler, combine, reconcile and exercise the diverse skills of businessman, lawyer, artist, engineer and advertising man, as well as those of author and journalist, psychiatrist, educator and psychologist. In what other profession can one expect better to observe the multifarious expressions of creativity?" MacKinnon's group of test subjects was culled from lists suggested by five professors of architecture who were asked to nominate the 40 most creative members of the profession at work in the United States.

One fact became apparent as the architects were studied: there was scarcely any connection between adult IQ and adult achievement. "It is clear," said MacKinnon, "that above a certain required minimum level of intelligence . . . being more intelligent does not guarantee a corresponding increase in creativeness. It just is not true that the more intelligent person is necessarily the more creative one."

MacKinnon found that many of his most creative subjects had taken a skeptical attitude toward formal education and had been utterly undistinguished in classes that did not interest them. A creative profile emerged. It showed a person much more willing to trust his intuition than the average, and ready to run risks. The creative architects exhibited wide-ranging interests, including many commonly classified as feminine. These and other traits reflected a highly developed sense of individualism, and MacKinnon's final portrait of the creative individual shows a person who is self-confident, uninhibited, outspoken, flexible, independent and strongly motivated. MacKinnon guessed that young students with creative potential probably had similar personality structures, though not so sharply etched as those of mature architects.

Finally, the study demonstrated a special pattern of upbringing among creative individuals. For one thing, families of the creative moved a great deal and this fact tended to set them apart from others in their neighborhoods. Further, MacKinnon says, "in almost every case in which the architect reported that his family differed in its behavior and values from those in the neighborhood, the family was different in showing greater cultural, artistic and intellectual interests and pursuits."

Parents generally had an "extraordinary respect for the child and confidence in his ability to do what was appropriate." MacKinnon says that "the expectation of the parent that the child would act independently but reasonably and responsibly appears to have contributed immensely to the latter's sense of personal autonomy which was to develop to such a marked degree." There was a lack of extreme emotional closeness between parents and children. But there was also a lack of over-dependency on the part of the children or severe rejection by the parents.

If MacKinnon suggested creativity was likely to flourish in families

Ingenuity gone awry

The 19th Century inventions pictured here share one thing in common—none of them work. Somewhere along the line the creative spark that led to their development misfired, and the far-flying, free-swinging imagination that is an essential ingredient in unconventional achievement generated only unconventional folly. By producing decidedly worthless contraptions, these inventors failed to bridge the gap between quaint contrivance and creativity.

Ensconced in a suitcase made of cork, the survivor of a shipwreck is depicted jauntily awaiting rescue, a testimonial to the inept ingenuity of the inventor.

Fire-Escape.

No. 221,855.   Patented Nov. 18, 1879.

This portable fire escape came complete with parachute and rubber-soled overshoes to absorb the shock of landing. But like many unwise ideas, this neck-stretching gadget never left the ground.

A horn-shaped ventilator was designed to filter fresh air into stuffy Victorian bedrooms. The inventor, a Belgian, went broke after customers complained of bumping their heads when rising in bed.

that were a bit "different," the research psychologist Victor Goertzel and his wife, Mildred, went even further in their book, *Cradles of Eminence*. They studied the childhoods and home environments of 400 creative men and women of this century. Surprisingly, the Goertzels' study found that a large percentage of the 400 came from troubled homes—homes where there was constant quarreling, where parents either rejected or dominated the children, or where one or both parents were absent because of divorce or death. In short, these were homes that might seem to have been breeding grounds for juvenile delinquents. The Goertzel study raises the question whether creators may be stung into creativity by a hunger for applause and love, and by a need to bury their problems in their creations. Freud apparently thought so; he held that the creative individual is neurotically maladjusted to society and that his work—every painting, verse or song—is just one sublimated urge transformed by the creative act. This view has long been popular, and there may be a good deal of truth in it for some persons. But individual variations being what they are, what holds for one does not hold for all. For every tormented Kafka or Dostoevski, there is a Thomas Mann or Victor Hugo whose life is a monument of creative and personal order.

While the MacKinnon and Goertzel studies show that home and family influence the creative personality, neither tries to answer a parallel question: What influence does society have? Some societies have produced staggering amounts of creative work of the very highest quality, among them Athens in the Fifth Century B.C., Renaissance Florence and Elizabethan London. Did they have anything in common that might explain why they were such fertile nurturing grounds for genius?

First of all, there was a climate of creativity. The people of the three cities all firmly believed that they were building new and better—more cultivated, more enlightened—forms of civilization, having only recently emerged (as they saw it) from a benighted age. Members of the first wave of towering Florentine artists, for example—the painter Giotto, the sculptors Donatello and Ghiberti, and the architect Brunelleschi—were all quite consciously rebelling against the stiff conventions of medieval art in creating a new, more humane and lifelike art of their own. That Shakespeare was also deliberately creating a new and better—more realistic, more subtle—drama seems clear from the play scene in *Hamlet*, in which Shakespeare pointedly chides the hammy acting of the visiting performers and the clumsy play they put on.

Another possible key to the power of some societies to inspire creativity is their size. Athens, Florence and London were, by today's standards, quite small. If it is not true that all the citizens knew one another, at least they were all aware of everything significant that went on in the town. All Athenian citizens attended the theater during the great spring drama festivals where the works of Aeschylus, Sophocles, Euripides and Aristophanes were performed. Studies of Shakespeare's audience indicate a passionate city-wide interest in drama; everyone from bricklayers to belted earls patronized the Globe theater to see Shakespeare's latest hit. In short, the artists had a savvy and appreciative audience to encourage them.

And evidence suggests that the artists themselves, while they were often personal friends, were extremely competitive, shamelessly swiping and then building on one another's innovations, each trying to outdo the others in perfecting his art. Shakespeare adopted and then modulated the thundering blank verse of Christopher Marlowe; Donatello's successor Verrocchio improved on Donatello's technical discoveries; and Michelangelo studied Verrocchio's work.

These sketchy portraits of Athens, Florence and London in their periods of superb creativity suggest parallels with the profile MacKinnon draws of the family backgrounds of his creative architects, although no such analogy can be stretched very far. In all three cities there was an atmosphere of intellectual ferment; in MacKinnon's families there was lively interest in artistic and intellectual pursuits. The families gave their children a sense of self-worth, of independence; the three cities were exuberantly self-confident and must have communicated this feeling to their citizens. The cities were restlessly developing what they saw as new civilizations—uninhibitedly, outspokenly testing new ways of living, just as the creative architects' families encouraged them to be flexible, to experiment, to forge ahead on their own.

Since special characteristics seem to go with a high level of creativity, it should be possible to identify creative people with tests. A number of schemes for measuring creative potential have been devised since World War II, but their effectiveness is yet to be proved. Most creativity tests derive from the work of Professor J. P. Guilford of the University of Southern California, who, in the early 1950s, devised examinations for the Office of Naval Research. The tests developed by Guilford and others probe for free-ranging imagination, covering areas like ideational fluency (list different uses for a common object like a barrel or a brick); word fluency (within an allotted time period, think of as many words as you can that rhyme with a given word); flexibility (find geometric figures embedded in complex patterns); and originality (write down the words brought to mind by a given word).

The "brick" test for ideational fluency shows how these tests work in practice. British psychologist Liam Hudson tested a group of English boys by asking them to think up all the uses that could be made of such simple, everyday objects as a brick, a barrel and a blanket. He was looking for amusing or novel responses.

One of the boys, a youth named Florence who was studying to be a scientist, suggested only two uses for a brick—to make a building or to smash a shopwindow in a robbery. At the other extreme was a boy named Poole, who was studying to be a linguist. He, too, mentioned the construction and missile uses, but then went on to suggest dueling—"bricks at ten paces, turn and throw; no evasive action allowed"—and tying bricks to the cor-

Picasso's fish: from lunch to art

The inspiration for some of the most original works of creativity has cropped up in the least expected places, a fact Picasso often took delight in demonstrating. By drawing from materials at hand, he fashioned a goat from a wicker basket, a palm frond and two milk pitchers. At another time, he sculptured a bull's head out of bicycle parts. But one of the most famous of his conversions of the mundane into art took place at a lunch and was recorded in the unusual photographs on these pages.

As Picasso picked at the bony remains of his luncheon sole *(opposite)*, an idea suddenly occurred to him. He leaped from the table and disappeared into his studio, returning a moment later with moist clay.

The sequence of photographs below shows how Picasso then gently lifted the fish skeleton from his plate and pressed it into the soft clay. Once the bones were imbedded he pulled them free, leaving fossil-like impressions, which he sliced from the clay with his pocketknife. Next he daubed a platter with paint and laid two of the clay fish on the plate. The design ready for firing, Picasso sat back to admire his creative inspiration.

ners of a comforter to keep it from slipping off a bed. Poole was even more inventive in his uses for a barrel, listing such far-out notions as placing the barrel on a fast phonograph turntable to spin-dry clothes ("water out through the bunghole").

Florence was much more down to earth than Poole. He figured, sensibly enough, that barrels were good for holding liquids and might come in handy at parties, as in the song "Roll out the Barrel." When the same questions were asked about a blanket, Florence, again very sensibly, figured a blanket was useful at bedtime and, hosed down, for putting out a small fire. Poole's inventive uses for a blanket included making smoke signals, serving "as a target for shooting practice for short-sighted people," providing a cover for lovemaking in the woods, catching people jumping out of burning buildings and doubling as a sail. After the sprightly Poole, Florence comes across as something of a wet blanket himself. Hudson drew no conclusions from the study, but it would seem obvious that Poole is more likely to be a creative person.

A different type of test was devised by Michael A. Wallach of Duke University and Nathan Kogan of the New School for Social Research, who set out to gauge not only the ability to generate ideas, but also the aptitude for producing unique ideas. One question asked children to name all the round things they could think of. Such obvious answers as "button," "plate" and "doorknob" scored points only for quantity, while unusual answers like "mousehole" and "drops of water" scored for uniqueness. Similarly, "wheelbarrow" and "trolley car" were not unique answers to the problem, "Name all the things you can think of that move on wheels." Only one child came up with the response "clothesline," while another imaginative fifth grader said "tape recorder."

Wallach and Kogan found that children who produced larger numbers of ideas also produced more unique ideas. The pattern was generally consistent from test to test and the results showed no relationship to the children's IQ scores. This suggested that the measurement was indeed getting at creativity rather than intelligence.

In contrast to the limited success of creativity testing are the promising results of some attempts to stimulate creativity. Today, there is an imperative for individuals to be creative—or, at least, to be thought to be creative. The methods for developing creativity are not mysterious. They simply aim to stretch minds by presenting tasks that require novelty, ingenuity and imagination—solving puzzles, painting pictures, composing stories and poems. The methods work best, understandably, under the stimulus of an outstanding teacher. As one advocate of these methods, Richard S. Crutchfield of the University of California, has concluded, "It goes without saying that methods which are intended to *teach* creative thinking must themselves *be* creative."

An example of the rich results that can be achieved by the kind of teachers Crutchfield has in mind appears in the work of poet Kenneth Koch. Koch has taught third through sixth graders in New York's Public School

61 both to read and to appreciate great adult poetry and, especially, to write poetry of their own. He had noticed that when children were given paper and crayons they became intensely excited—and creative. Why not try the same with words?

Koch started off by creating as relaxed a classroom atmosphere as he could and then suggested a simple formula to get the children writing, a formula such as "I wish. . . ." or "I remember . . . but I forget. . . ." To help break down inhibitions, Koch also urged the children to be "silly" and "crazy." The results have been astonishing, including these haunting lines by a fifth-grade student:

> *I remember knowing how a magician made me,*
> *But I forget how it used to be in the dustland.*

Another young poet, Argentina Wilkerson, a fourth grader, put down her thoughts about airplanes: "I wish planes had motors that went rum bang zingo and would be streaming green as the sea." A sixth grader named Hipolito Rivera, having read William Blake's "Tyger! Tyger! burning bright," imagined instead a giraffe:

> *Giraffe! Giraffe!*
> *What kicky, sticky legs you've got.*
> *What a long neck you've got.*
> *It looks like a stick of fire.*

And Arnaldo Gomez, age 11, found love:

> *Two people in love are like two rockets blasting off to the same planet.*
> *Two people in love are like the two of them floating free of gravity.*
> *Two people in love are like light against light, all becoming as one.*
> *Two people in love are like two stars put together turning into one planet.*
> *Love is like thunder and lightning going through one planet.*
> *Love is like two planets turning into the size of stars, then becoming as one.*

That such imaginative imagery was born in the heart and mind of a child once again emphasizes the ultimate mystery of creativity. While the encouragement of a gifted teacher like Koch can help to release it, only the inimitable essence of a small individual named Arnaldo Gomez could have fashioned the poem in just that way.

Steps in the creative process

The creative process is as highly personal and individualistic as the individuals who do the creating. But at one time or another, all creative people must go through essentially the same steps: they find sources of inspiration, express their ideas, reflect on them and refine them to the point of fruition.

Before worthwhile and original work can begin, the creator must master the skills necessary to express his ideas. Most creative people, like the seven-year-old children practicing ballet at Vienna's State Opera House in the picture opposite, begin to develop their special abilities early—Picasso was a better painter than his art-teacher father while still a schoolboy. But some remarkable talents, like the famous 19th Century photographer Julia Margaret Cameron, have not turned to creative activity until middle age.

The sheer labor of preparing for creative activity can be awesome. The 19th Century American painter Thomas Eakins was so obsessed with achieving lifelike reality in his portraits that he took courses in anatomy at a medical college and dissected cadavers to enhance his knowledge of the human body. The value of such painstaking preparation was hinted at by the painter Vincent Van Gogh in a letter to his brother Theo. "In my opinion," he wrote, "an artist must not spare himself when it goes hard. So much is gained that he harvests his studies just as the farmer harvests his crops."

Once the harvest of skills is in, the creator can begin to put it to use, realizing his potential through the steps of the creative process. And no matter what medium he chooses to work in, the stamp of his individuality ultimately distinguishes his work.

Young dancers aspiring to roles in Vienna's ballet corps view their progress in mirrors as their teacher claps cadence for their steps.

Inspired by clippings that clutter the floor and cover the walls, James Rosenquist paints billboard-sized canvases.

Conception

The inspiration for creative achievement can come from almost any source. Pop artist James Rosenquist (*opposite*) is stimulated by the illustrations littering his studio. Jazzmen Gerry Mulligan and Dave Brubeck (*below*) derive ideas by listening to each other.

Ideas often pop up unconsciously. Photographer Diane Arbus discovered that when she gazed at the pictures on her bedroom walls, "a subliminal thing" aroused her creative impulse.

Gerry Mulligan (left) and Dave Brubeck interact as they improvise at a jazz concert.

A young artist eagerly attacks her work during a program run by New York's Museum of Modern Art.

Italian moviemaker Federico Fellini approaches his work with a symphony conductor's zest while directing the cast of his film "Satyricon."

Execution

There are many individualistic ways of attacking a creative problem. The uninhibited artist at left approaches the canvas with bold, confident strokes. But for others, an empty canvas, a formless lump of clay, a blank sheet of paper can be a terrifying experience.

The novelist Henry Miller begins his writing "in absolute chaos and darkness, in a bog or swamp of ideas. . . ." Still others, like filmmaker Federico Fellini *(above)* seem to revel in the unknown. "There are two ways to make films," Fellini explains. "One, you prepare well in advance. In this way you plan everything and you lose enthusiasm. . . . The second way, you prepare in a vague sort of sense and then you begin. This way is more fun."

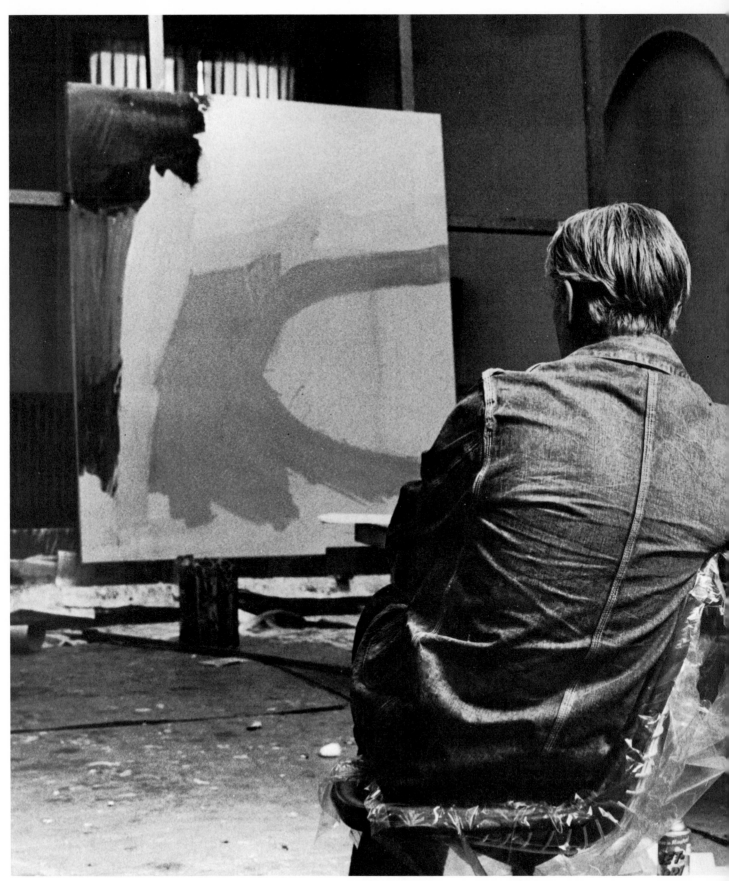

Willem de Kooning contemplates one of his abstract paintings. If it fails to satisfy him at this point, he may abandon or even destroy it.

Appraisal

Even the most inventive and confident individuals go through periods of examining and refining their works as they struggle to realize their creative insights. D. H. Lawrence once wrote the same novel three times before he was finally satisfied. Picasso ceaselessly reworked his paintings until the moment when they were framed.

The Dutch-born abstract expressionist Willem de Kooning *(left)* works in flashes of feverish activity separated by long periods of contemplation and revision. He spent two years on one canvas, painting it out hundreds of times. "It's like shooting dice," he says. "I shoot ten and then try again. I just keep throwing till I get what I want."

The result

Removed from the sweat and litter of the studio, the finished work takes on a life of its own, inviting all who behold it to ponder its meaning. Sometimes, as shown here, the public reaction may be one of puzzlement.

The originality of a creative work can make its worth difficult to recognize, and the authors of some of mankind's greatest achievements have died before their work was appreciated. Gregor Mendel's laws of heredity had to be rediscovered after his death, while Vincent Van Gogh sold but one painting to the public—for about $80—before he killed himself. Thus public understanding of a work—the ultimate step in the creative process—often proves to be beyond the creator's control.

Intrigued and mystified by Alexander Calder's puzzling "Black Widow" sculpture, two women move up close to seek its significance.

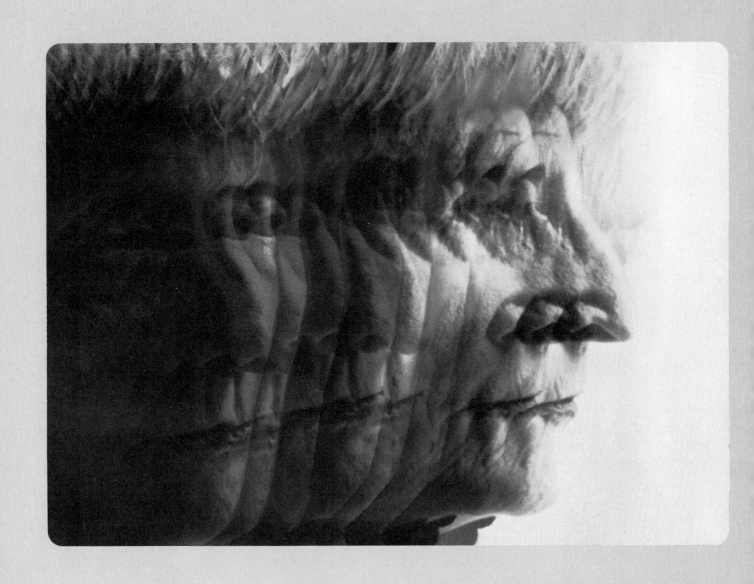

The Personality Enigma

5

No person likes to think of himself as average. He resents being stereotyped, labeled like a specimen in a museum case. He insists that no single label can do justice to the complex person he really is. Yet often he does not hesitate to pin labels on others. His boss is tyrannical, one of his co-workers is phony, a friend is a square shooter. Such typecasting is a kind of quick personality analysis that helps people keep a character-reference file on those they know. It simplifies the problem of identifying and coping with others, and predicting how they will behave, just as brand names in a supermarket are guides to product dependability.

But there is a serious flaw in treating human beings like canned goods, and it derives from the nature of personality and human behavior. For people are often not what they seem at first sight, or second or third sight. It takes many sightings to get a complete view of the elusive, shifting quality called personality—even photographers trying to capture the essence of an individual on film often use multiple exposures, as the noted British photographer Cecil Beaton did for his portrait of Dame Edith Sitwell, the novelist and poet *(opposite)*. The reason personality is so hard to pin down is simple: the behavior of any individual on one occasion may be —or at least appear to be—wholly inconsistent with the behavior of that same person in a different situation. Consider the following scenario:

The scene is a room filled with typists clattering away at their machines and junior executives chattering into telephones. In the foreground, standing by a water cooler are a man and a woman. The man, John Wilson, is in his mid-twenties, gangly, slouching and indifferently dressed. To his right is Frances Beasely, a roly-poly woman in a bright-pink dress and pink cheeks to match, and a heavily lipsticked mouth that is usually wide open, either talking or laughing. Just now she is waving an invitation to another secretary, Betsy Lynd, to join them at the water cooler. Betsy is sitting at her desk outside the closed door of an executive office. A slight figure wearing a plain-Jane skirt and sweater, she gives a diffident smile, shakes her head "No," and looks down at her work, avoiding Wilson's attempt to catch her eye. At that moment the door behind her desk opens and Roger Clendan, the office manager, emerges. He is a tall, husky man in his early fifties, well dressed and meticulously barbered.

Stepping purposefully over to the secretary, he thrusts a large manila file folder under her nose. "Miss Lynd, what file did I ask you for?"

Betsy's voice is low and deferential as she replies, "The Waterman file, Mr. Clendan."

"And what file is *this?*" Clendan asks, biting off each word.

Betsy peers at the identifying tag on the outside. "Isn't it the . . . oh my, Waterbury. I'm sorry." She rises and scurries to the file cabinet. Clendan puffs out his chest like a general who has just routed an enemy column and marches back to his office. Before he steps through the door, he notices John Wilson and Frances Beasely at the water cooler. The two have their heads bent toward each other, apparently laughing at a private joke.

"Wilson!" Clendan shouts across the room. "My understanding is that you're supposed to work at a desk, not at a water cooler."

John flushes and looks around him, as if for support. "I was just—"

Without waiting for the reply, Clendan glares briefly at Frances, turns on his heel, enters his office and slams the door.

"I was only here a minute, wasn't I?" John asks, as much to the room at large as to his companion.

Frances starts to laugh again. "Don't let him scare you. Clendan gets paid to stick his head out of his door once an hour and crow about something—just like a cuckoo clock." Betsy hurries by with an armful of filing folders, and Frances calls out sympathetically: "Did he chew you out too, dear?" But Betsy is preoccupied and she rushes on without saying a word.

At first glance, all four people in this scenario seem to be stereotypes. Roger Clendan is the classic bully—aggressive, self-confident, physically imposing, determined to succeed in spite of others. Frances Beasely is the mythical, jolly fat person, outgoing, amiable, with a heart as big as her bosom. John Wilson is the eternal loser, physically awkward, personally unsure, seeking but never quite getting the approval of others. And Betsy Lynd is the professional self-denier, the kind of person who rigidly follows the rules and avoids personal contact when possible.

This instant typecasting seems satisfactory as a way to describe the personalities of the people in the office confrontation. But suppose they are observed again a few hours later, at the end of the day. Roger Clendan is slouched in the family car, being driven home from a suburban railroad station by his wife. His voice is subdued as he describes a meeting in which his department head announced a reorganization no one had consulted him about. His wife breaks in: "I warned you they were after your job, but you wouldn't believe me. You always trust people too much and let them push you around."

John Wilson, meanwhile, is spending an evening with friends. He is playing darts for beers, and beating each challenger. A small crowd has gathered to watch; one pretty girl smiles admiringly as he throws his third bull's-eye. He catches her glance and says, "Want a quick lesson?" She smiles. He faces the dart board and tosses another bull's-eye.

At about this time, Frances Beasely is sitting alone in her apartment yelling into the phone at her cleaning woman. She has come home to discover that the refrigerator has not been defrosted and the breakfast dishes have not been washed. There is an edge of hysteria as she says, "I'll be damned if I'll work all day to pay you to sit around doing nothing. I've been too good to you and that's why you think you can take advantage. . . ."

Meanwhile, Betsy Lynd rehearses with a little theater group. She is playing a love scene; her face is radiant, her thin body moving gracefully. With a few words, a gesture, a tilt of her head, she charges the room with the power of her stage personality. The mousey office girl has metamorphosed into a brilliant stage creature.

These examples are clearly invented to make a point. But the careful observer of people will expect just such unexpected changes of character in real life. People cannot be classified easily. Stereotypes may do in Hollywood: the movie-goer can predict that John Wayne will be strong and manly in his next film. But real people behave in apparently contradictory ways. A Frances Beasely can be both warm-hearted and mean. Roger Clendan's office bombast may collapse before the authority of his wife.

As difficult as it is to define and measure such basic human attributes as intelligence and creativity, it is even harder to pin down so complex a quality as personality. For one thing, the shifting psychological picture rests on a physical base. Everything from endocrine glands to diet may affect personality in ways that the individual himself cannot anticipate or control. An overactive thyroid, for example, can cause insomnia and irritability, or an underactive thyroid can make the individual sluggish and unemotional. As a poet once sang dyspeptically: *My soul is dark with stormy riot/Directly traceable to diet.* And author Joseph Conrad spelled out the effect of digestion on personality: "The joy of life . . . depends on a sound stomach, whereas a bad digestion inclines one to skepticism, incredulity, breeds black fancies and thoughts of death."

Beyond these physical elements lies the fact that humans are such mixtures of animal emotion and rational thought that they often do not understand their own behavior. Novelist Arthur Koestler has described these two sides of man's make-up: "Emotion and reason when not in acute conflict, lead an agonized coexistence. On one side, the pale cast of rational thought, of logic suspended on a thin thread all too easily broken; on the other, the native fury of passionately held irrational beliefs."

The proliferation of personality theories in this century may represent an attempt to reconcile what Koestler feels is a presently unreconcilable human condition. The term personality itself commonly refers to the external impression a person makes—meek like Betsy Lynd, sternly strong like Roger Clendan. But this appearance is so often misleading that psychologists often apply the word personality to internal and external qualities together, the sum of what a person is—not just the way he appears to the world and even to himself, but a personal essence, the real individual beneath the layers of social armor. Few people know even their closest friends in this way. Great writers, great painters or great lovers

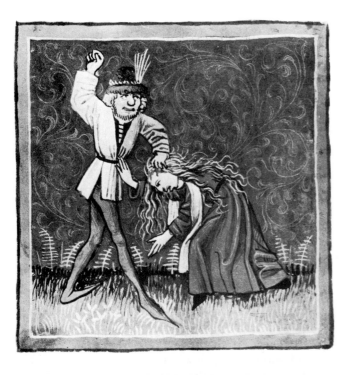

may occasionally come close. The average person, lacking insight into the complex factors that determine personality, settles for an approximation when he tries to characterize others'. He generally makes do with types in his daily life, fitting personalities to easy labels, as the simplest way to predict behavior.

From the first, the study of personality has sought a more satisfactory means of characterizing people and predicting behavior. The origin of the word personality itself suggests the difficulty. The root is Greek: *persona*, meaning mask. Greek actors of Pericles' day wore stylized masks that helped the audience recognize the characters represented. Off stage, of course, masks have usually been worn more to conceal than reveal. Sometimes this "public personality," as the great psychologist Carl Jung called it, dominates the individual. Jung went on to warn that the more a person identifies with the persona, the greater the risk that he will be alienated from his true self. The player becomes the role.

Through the ages, men have attempted to see through the mask. The simplest—and some of the oldest—methods of character analysis try to relate the entire personality to some fixed physical characteristic. In Western Europe, redheads are thought hot-tempered; a generous nature goes with a large nose in Italy, with a pot belly in Japan.

One of the most ancient tools for reading personality is the examination of handwriting: the 11th Century Chinese wrote learned commentaries on the subtle relationship between personality and calligraphy. Other methods of analysis have focused on habits and unconscious movements—the "body language" that everyone uses at some time or other. Perhaps the ultimate in these lines of reasoning was the attempt by 19th Century phrenologists to classify people according to the bumps on their skulls.

Modern psychologists also sometimes resort to physical appearances to explain personality. The respected Gordon Allport of Harvard, for example, believed that expressive posture, gait and handwriting comprise "an important (perhaps the most important) factor in our understanding of personality." He cited research that claimed a correlation between gestures and inner attitudes: "The open hand dangling between the legs . . . characteristically accompanies frustration; fingers folded at tips, suspicion or resignation; hand to nose, fear; finger to lips, shame; fist gestures, aggression; one finger enveloped by other hand, ego-inflation or encouragement."

Even the deeper efforts to explain personality sometimes seem unrelated and contradictory. In some cases the theorists' own backgrounds and individual sense of life seem to color their theories. W. H. Sheldon, the leading modern exponent of body conformation as a determinant of personality, was the son of an animal breeder. The originator of the inkblot test, Hermann Rorschach, was an art instructor's son who dabbled in ink sketches himself; it is of more than passing interest to discover that in high school Hermann was nicknamed *Kleck*, Swiss-German for inkblot.

The theories of personality that are now most important *(pages 134-145)* rest on one or another of a few fundamental concepts. These modern explorations of personality approach it from two different directions: from outside the individual, or from inside.

The external study of personality attempts through tests and interviews to organize the surface evidence more effectively, characterizing an individual by analyzing the way that he appears to himself and others. This approach goes beyond the crude labels that are used to type people, providing a list of personality traits that serve as a card file index to human behavior.

Sorting and filing traits began in the 1930s with Gordon Allport, perhaps the most influential of "trait theorists." Allport insisted that understanding personality required breaking it into elements. "The only thing you can do about total personality is to send flowers to it," he said. It was the parts that were important. With his colleague Henry S. Odbert, Allport compiled a list of 17,953 trait words from a dictionary; words like mean, generous, kind, spiteful, rude. He and his followers regarded these traits as pieces in the large mosaic of human personality.

The trait theorists argued endlessly about how to arrange the pieces, and about the origin and significance of traits. Allport himself pointed out that a seemingly similar trait in two persons may arise from different causes and have different effects. "Shyness in one person," he said, "may be due to hereditary influences that no amount of contrary pressure from the environment has been able to offset; in another person shyness may stem from an inferiority feeling built by an abnormally exacting environment. . . . Conversely, two youths suffering some shocking experience of grief or bitter disappointment, objectively alike, may be affected very differently. One of them becomes morose and ineffectual, lost in his trouble; the other stiffens his back and becomes more realistic and aggressive. The same fire that melts the butter, hardens the egg."

More recently, many psychologists have begun to question the meaning of traits. Experiments show that even a supposedly bedrock trait like honesty can be broken down into a spectrum of qualities. Each influences the others, and they all change with the situation. These developments have given rise to a new school of psychologists who believe traits are no more reliable as personality indicators than the stereotypes ordinary people use. These men maintain that the situation itself is more important in determining personality than inherent qualities of behavior.

Other psychologists take a different approach, examining personality not from the outside, but from within, following Sigmund Freud's lead. These psychoanalytical theorists think personality is determined at an early age by conflicts and instincts buried in the unconscious, a part of the human psyche beyond the awareness and control of the individual. Only by uncovering and dissecting these hidden feelings, they believe, can an individual's outer characteristics be explained.

Freud's famous colleague, Alfred Adler, was one of the most influential supporters of this view. Adler believed that personality can be crippled at an early age. He suggested three great cripplers: a feeling of inferiority

The ancient pseudo science of astrology, recently enjoying a resurgence of popularity, links personality to the zodiac. This is an imaginary belt of stars divided into 12 signs that are symbolized by mythical creatures, as shown in the large circle in this 18th Century engraving. The zodiac rotates, bringing a different sign overhead for each part of the year. An individual born under the sign of Taurus (the Bull) is held to be stubborn, one born under Leo (the Lion), generous.

(he invented the concept of the inferiority complex), parental neglect and parental pampering. He put great stock in the importance of birth order, claiming that the first-born, once the center of attention, might react with lifelong feelings of insecurity and hatred of others when dethroned by the second-born. He also theorized that first-borns are obsessed with the past and that they often become neurotics or drunkards. By contrast, he saw the second child as ambitious, trying to outdo the older sibling. The third-born, he maintained, was likely to be spoiled and so smothered with affection that he would grow into a maladjusted adult.

The different approaches to personality study are reflected in the tests widely used to sketch portraits of human personalities and to provide a basis for predicting how different individuals will behave. The interior approach, based on Freud's theory that the source of personality lies in the unconscious, is reflected by the projective tests that ask the subject to project his personality by bringing unconscious ideas to the surface. The exterior approach utilizes objective tests that relate directly to surface characteristics, but in the process may tap unconscious areas. Each type of test uses a different material and seeks a different response from the individual being examined. (For a personal account of what it is like to be tested this way, see pages 124-125.)

In objective tests the subject gives yes-no, true-false or multiple-choice answers to specific questions. The answers provide a self-report inventory of personality—the subject's own estimations of himself. The best-known objective test is the Minnesota Multiphasic Personality Inventory (MMPI). In past years it was widely administered in schools and industry, but is now used mainly to evaluate prison inmates and clinic patients;

however, somewhat similar tests, such as the Strong Vocational Interest Blank and the California Psychological Inventory, continue to be used in examining students, corporate employees and job applicants.

The MMPI is a questionnaire that asks the subject to mark as True or False 550 statements such as "I daydream very little"; "My mother or father made me obey even when I thought it was unreasonable"; "I am worried about sex matters"; "When I get bored I like to stir up some excitement"; "I sometimes think I am losing my mind."

Unlike IQ test questions, those on the MMPI have no correct answers. Each subject's responses are evaluated by comparison with those of other subjects. The test may be compared with previous examples to help predict whether a prisoner can be paroled or a mental patient released.

The other type of evaluation, the projective test, gives the subject almost complete freedom in answering, merely prompting him to release thoughts he may have suppressed. It is like a school essay test. The subject may be shown a picture or design and asked to say whatever comes to mind. Or he may have to perform a specific act such as drawing a figure or arranging blocks. The responses have no obvious relationship to personality—the subject is not reporting his own view of his characteristics as he is in an objective test—but such a relationship can be deduced by comparing responses from several people.

The most famous projective test is the Rorschach. The interviewer shows 10 inkblots: some are colored, some suggest textures, some resemble natural forms, some are fantastic in shape. The subject then tells what he sees in the blots—clouds, bugs, blood, humans, sexual objects or whatever. There are no standard answers, though many people see certain forms —bats, for example—in some blots.

In scoring a Rorschach, the interviewer places great emphasis on the subject's approach: Is he methodical or confused, creative or bizarre, aggressive or depressed. Although comparisons between answers to projective tests are less precise than comparisons in objective tests, they are still a key to interpretation. A bizarre response to a certain inkblot is not just one that makes the interviewer uneasy; it is a response that is rarely, if ever, given by normal people.

Partisans of the Rorschach test claim it provides a full personality profile if used by a skillful clinician. Others question its validity, however; among the deficiencies noted by critics is the variation in scoring among examiners. More serious, perhaps, is the difficulty in relating Rorschach responses to real behavior, that is, to see how this type of test predicts an individual's future actions. A good evaluation of the Rorschach is that of S. J. Beck, a proponent of the tests. Conclusions drawn from the Rorschach, he says, should be regarded "not as truths but as hypotheses."

So far as general predictive value is concerned, the objective tests have come in for their share of criticism as well. One serious weakness of such tests, especially when they are used to check out job, school or military-service applicants, is the possibility of faked responses. Often the subject can anticipate the interpretation the examiner will put on his answers. After all, someone trying to get into law school is not likely to respond affirmatively to the statement "I sometimes think I am losing my mind," although someone trying to escape Army service might willingly agree with that statement. To trip up the consistent liar, most objective tests include a few statements that apply to almost everyone, such as "I sometimes put off till tomorrow what I should do today." A negative response to such statements alerts the examiner to suspect faking.

Some objective tests try to prevent self-serving answers by requiring choices between statements that many people would find almost equally desirable or undesirable. The subject may be asked to select the more applicable sentence in a pair like this:

A. I feel like blaming others when things go wrong for me.

B. I feel I am inferior in most respects.

Only someone very familiar with test-scoring techniques can interpret replies to these queries. The very fact that the choice is subtle and forced raises questions. Critics say that forced-choice tests can distort the picture. One authority equated such questions to the old joke, "Do you still beat your wife?" The subject is damned whatever his answer.

M ost psychologists, if asked today how successful tests have been in characterizing personality, probably would say that their value is limited to screening mentally disturbed people from the rest of the population. When it comes to predicting the day-to-day behavior of normal people, they would say that the tests are not very successful.

This conclusion is borne out by experience with the MMPI, which has been given to hundreds of thousands of people whose personal characteristics were known from other sources—hospital records, prison records, school records, in-depth interviews. Researchers have therefore had ample opportunity to seek correlations between patterns of behavior and responses to groups of MMPI items. The correlation is excellent—the test works reliably—when the MMPI is used to distinguish between categories of mentally disturbed people. But attempts to measure normal traits with the MMPI—and with items from other objective tests—have led into a thicket of difficulties. The results simply were not reliable.

In spite of these limitations, personality tests are now more widely used, in the United States at least, than ever before. There are about 600 different tests and they are taken by millions of people every year. Often the tests are not called personality tests, but adjustment scales, interest or attitude inventories, or occupational-preference surveys. These varied names are not simply euphemisms intended to conceal personality assessments, but are rather an indication of a different focus.

The tests are most frequently used by school guidance counselors, college deans and corporation personnel managers. They are not attempting to predict day-to-day human behavior with great precision or to make an exact science out of the study of human personality. Instead, they are try-

On the firing line in a battery of tests

While writing this book the author put his own personality to the test. He arranged to undergo three different kinds of evaluations; segments of the three tests that he took are shown below at left. The first of the three tests was a drawing exercise, designed to reveal parts of the unconscious personality. Next came the Wechsler Adult Intelligence Scale, a portion of which requires that the subject copy, using colored blocks, patterns from a small notebook. The last was the famous Rorschach test, in which the subject projects his personality through his spontaneous reactions to a set of inkblots.

The process of taking the tests proved something of a psychological experience in itself, as author Good explains in the report that appears herewith.

The drawings the author made for one personality test resembled these that he sketched later. The originals, easy for the layman to misinterpret, are kept confidential by the psychologist.

One part of the Wechsler IQ test gave Good nine colored blocks, with which he duplicated a pattern in a book. The subtest helps assess visual-motor ability and reasoning in spatial relationships.

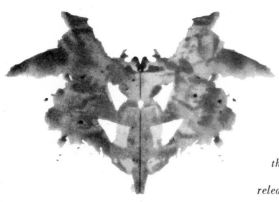

This inkblot is one of the 10 used in the test developed by Swiss psychiatrist Hermann Rorschach to prompt the release of unconscious thoughts. This blot, and others, suggested a bat to Good.

The pretty clinician who was in charge of administering the tests had warned me that ethics precluded giving a person the results of either the figure-drawing test or the Wechsler intelligence test—results which under normal circumstances would be given to a psychologist or some other professional. She then explained that sometimes potentially disturbing information was developed. I blithely replied that at my stage of the game nothing new I could learn about myself would surprise me. That self-confidence lasted for approximately 30 seconds, until the moment when the clinician gave me her first order:

"Please draw a person."

This was rather unnerving for someone whose drawing ability has not visibly improved since the age of nine or 10, when it was awful even for a child. I felt I was about to reveal a kind of artistic illiteracy, a juvenile atavism that would unmask the bright, urbane, middle-aged fellow who was taking the test. Furthermore her order required a sexual choice of me. What kind of a person did she want me to draw? And what conclusion would she come to from my choice? I plunged ahead with a sketch of a man, a lopsided and rather juvenile looking creature with too-long arms and tiny hands.

"All right," she continued, "now draw a picture of a woman."

My libido opted for a glorious, opulent nude, but my hand was bringing forth something that might well have been put together by my seven-year-old daughter. My hand, I noticed, was sweating. Now that was absurd. I had come to take a personality and not an art test. But why was she looking so closely at each awkward detail—the moplike hair, the fingers like a bunch of green beans?

Obviously, my man and my woman would not be judged for artistic quality, but for omissions I made and details I included. However, a person who is a ludicrous drawer may do a careless and even an incomplete job simply because (as was the case with me) he has learned over the years that lavishing time and attention will little improve the wretched product of his artistic toil. I began to wonder if the assignment I had been given was actually a ploy to throw the test subject off balance at the very start.

When I turned to the Wechsler test, my annoyance grew. I was faced with a variety of tasks, one of them that of copying two-dimensional geometric patterns from a book with a set of bi-colored blocks. My desire to do well after the drawing debacle was countered by an abiding aversion to anything that smacks of geometry. I felt that I had been lured into an unfair game. Professor Wechsler might extract portentous intellectual meaning from my performance, but I was convinced that it was revealing very little more than an aptitudinal predisposition (or lack of it) such as that which enables one child to sing like a nightingale and causes another to sing like an owl. In the midst of these reflections, as the blocks slid back and forth beneath my hands, I wondered why my palms persistently remained clammy.

The next portion, I felt, made both scientific and common sense. The clinician read aloud a long list of paired words and urged me to comment on their similarities. Asked, for example, how "reward" and "blame" were alike, I replied, "Both are the results of human activity." I learned that I had scored zero for that one on a scale of zero, one or two.

Professor Wechsler graciously permits you to try again if you do not succeed at first, but my second attempt was even worse: "Good elicits a reward—bad, blame." What was wrong with these answers? The clinician explained that the first one was too general, while the second one was at once too concrete and not satisfying the instruction to find similarities. A proper two-point answer might be, "A means of motivating," which correctly applies to both words. It seemed to me that my answer indicated at least some personality conflict over the concept of praise and blame.

Interpretations of the Rorschach inkblot test are more esoteric. I had read a good deal about this test before taking it. Bats are a popular form seen by many subjects in the fantastic inkblots. Whether or not the power of suggestion was operating, I seemed to see a great many bats on the first three cards. I wondered if some could be coming from my belfry.

I was pleased when at last I saw something different: a rabbit.

"There is a bunny," I said.

"A what?" she asked.

"A bunny, a rabbit," I replied. Too late I realized that the word bunny, used whimsically in our family, might be interpreted as an eccentric mode of thinking.

Why else was the clinician writing furiously on her sheet? Cautionary signals began sounding. Although she encouraged me to find as many things as I could on each card, I wondered at what point my natural responses were being supplemented by forced responses to satisfy authority's request for multiple interpretations of the inkblots.

I saw in the blots a profusion of humanoid masks or forms, crablike creatures, two puppies very nearly, but not quite, nuzzling each other. When the clinician and I discussed her findings, she told me that the puppies that were not quite nuzzling indicated strong but unsatisfied affectional needs. Maybe so. But could not my answer just as readily be interpreted to indicate a history of satisfied affectional needs that led me to see the puppies on the verge of obtaining such satisfaction themselves?

She reported that the number of masks that I had identified in the Rorschach blots suggested a preoccupation with the outward appearance of things and people because of inner conflicts that blocked the full expression of drives and abilities. This was possible, even probable, and I give the Rorschach test a high grade in perception on this point.

Finally, when all three of the tests were completed, I was nagged by a conviction reminiscent of school-day post-examination feelings that I should have done better. After all, there was so much that I knew about the subject—myself—that I had not even begun to have a chance to tell.

ing to get a line on their students, employees or clients for various reasons: gauging children's readiness for school, counseling married couples, providing career advice, screening and promoting workers. One corporation tests its top executives, then tests the lower ranks and compares results in considering individuals for promotion. Many organizations find these tests useful, but critics challenge this conclusion.

The screening of job applicants with personality tests has aroused the same objection that is directed against a similar application of general intelligence tests *(page 80)*—characteristics unrelated to the job should not disqualify an applicant. This view has now been given the force of law in the United States by the Supreme Court: tests may legally be used for job-related purposes, but not for general fishing expeditions to find out what somebody is like. Thus, an applicant for a job in a bank could not legally be tested for kindness or generosity, but he could be tested for honesty. That is, he could if there were a reliable test for honesty. There is not. The problem is not the law but the inadequacy of the trait of honesty. The concept is so complex and so vague that there is no guarantee that an applicant who passed any existing test would be honest in every situation.

It is this difficulty—the inability of traits to predict behavior consistently—that has led a growing number of psychologists to abandon reliance on traits. Among the growing number of psychologists who believe it is fruitless to try to explain behavior in terms of personality traits is Walter Mischel of Stanford University. Mischel acknowledges the existence of ingrained characteristics, but believes that what a person brings to a situation is less important in determining what he will do than the situation itself. "Obviously," Mischel writes, "people have characteristics. . . . Obviously, knowing how a person behaved before can help predict how he will behave again in similar contexts." He cites a homely example: "The individual who knows how to be assertive with waiters . . . or who knows how to solve certain kinds of interpersonal problems competently, or who excels in singing is *capable* of such performances enduringly." But, Mischel adds, "What people do in any situation may be changed dramatically even by relatively trivial alterations in their prior experiences or by slight modifications in the particular features of the immediate situation."

Situational theorists like Mischel believe people are predictable, but only in the context of specific activities and environments. Instead of labeling a person with a list of traits, these psychologists limit themselves to describing what that person will do in certain roles: employee, parent, lover, friend. If the circumstances surrounding a particular role change, so presumably will the behavior. Of all the situational factors that can bring about such changes, none is more potent than the continuous give-and-take between the individual and his fellows. The classic experiments backing this idea were those conducted between 1928 and 1930 by Hugh Hartshorne and Mark A. May of Columbia University. They studied the honesty of thousands of school children in an attempt to find out how many would cheat if given the chance and how many would remain honest no matter what the temptation.

The results indicated that there was no such thing as consistently honest or dishonest behavior. Nearly all of the children cheated when they thought they could get away with it. The basic design of the experiment was simple. The children were given intelligence and achievement tests; their test scores were noted by the experimenters in ways that the children were not aware of; then the children were given a chance to grade themselves on how well they had done. After one classroom test, papers were collected, the children's answers transcribed and the papers returned. Then the teacher read the correct answers and each child was supposed to mark his own paper. If the child changed any of his wrong answers to improve his grade, the deception was immediately apparent.

Hartshorne and May found to their surprise that they were unable to divide the children into clearly defined groups of cheaters and noncheaters. Instead, moderate cheating was the norm. If any children had an ingrained aversion to doing something dishonest, it was barely detectable. For the most part, the rate of cheating varied from test to test according to three factors: the risk involved, the effort required and the behavior of others in the class. In nearly every case this study showed that the trait of honesty in children could be bent almost beyond recognition by the situation.

Later research suggested that ethical behavior becomes more firmly established in individuals as they get older. But two ingenious experiments with adult subjects have offered further evidence that many people will readily alter ingrained behavioral patterns under pressure from those they consider their equals or their superiors.

In one of these experiments, Solomon Asch, then at Swarthmore College, showed how insidious peer-group pressure can be. Eight college students were seated together in a room and allowed to examine two white cards. The first card had a single vertical line on it. The second card had three vertical lines—one was exactly the same length as the line on the first card, while the other two lines were markedly longer or shorter. Each subject was supposed to judge for himself which line on the second card was equal to the line on the first card, and then announce his decision aloud. The catch was that all but one member of the group were confederates of the experimenter who had told them what to say in advance. On the first few trials, the confederates behaved normally, giving the correct answers when presented with each pair of cards. But then the confederates began to give incorrect answers, identifying lines that were obviously too long or too short as equal to the line on the first card. Round after round, the subject found himself in the role of the lone dissenter. His eyes told him one thing; the other seven people in the room kept telling him something else. Would he stick to his own judgment in the face of unanimous opposition? Or would he conform to the majority opinion?

The differences between the lines were so great—as much as seven inches in some cases—that Asch's subject almost never made an error when

The Viennese physician Josef Breuer is remembered today chiefly because he used hypnosis to treat the hallucinations of a young woman he called Anna O.— the case that led Sigmund Freud into his initial work in psychoanalysis.

Pioneer probers of the unconscious

Until the late 19th Century, the well-springs of personality were largely unexplored. Then men like Josef Breuer *(above)* in Vienna and Jean-Martin Charcot *(right)* in Paris began to probe for hidden influences on behavior, frequently using a technique that had formerly been shunned by serious medical men as a stage trick: hypnosis.

In a hypnotic trance a person may recall experiences that he has apparently forgotten. Charcot and other physicians of the time suspected that what was said under hypnotism was not meaningless gibberish but an expression of thoughts in a previously unexplored part of the mind. By using hypnotism to reach this hidden realm, later termed the unconscious, these pioneers were able in many cases to relieve anxieties and effect at least a partial cure of patients' neuroses. Their methods are rarely used now, but their perception of the significance of the unconscious paved the way for later discoveries.

The influence of Breuer and Charcot on modern personality theory became important by chance. Late in 1882, Breuer described one of his cases to the Viennese neurologist Sigmund Freud. And in the winter of 1885-1886, Freud was among the enthralled observers at one of Charcot's demonstrations. His imagination fired, Freud began to study neuroses and was led to the discovery of psychoanalysis and a whole new way of looking at personality.

In a dramatic moment at the Salpêtrière hospital in Paris, Jean-Martin Charcot (right) demonstrates the curative power of hypnosis.

the confederates did not lie. He had no difficulty selecting lines of equal length, so long as no one contradicted him. But when the confederates began to play their tricks, his decision-making began to disintegrate. If the confederates chose a wrong answer, so did the lone subject in a large proportion of the trials. Not all the subjects gave in. But three quarters of them denied the evidence of their senses at least once, and some individuals surrendered to the majority in trial after trial. In a later experiment, Asch provided the subject with a single "partner," who always answered correctly no matter what the other confederate did. This support stiffened the spine of most subjects, and their errors were reduced by three fourths.

It can be argued that judging the length of a line is a trivial exercise, that subjects who altered traits following cues from the crowd were simply refusing to argue publicly over a minor point. But this argument does not begin to account for the results of studies conducted by Stanley Milgram at Yale in the 1960s. Milgram challenged his subjects on the deepest level—and brought to light shocking proof of the shift in basic personality characteristics under pressure of authority.

Milgram describes his experiments in his book *Obedience to Authority*. The authority is an experimenter who tells the volunteer subjects he is studying "the effects of punishment on learning." The subjects are instructed to give what they believe to be painful electrical shocks to a "learner," who is supposed to be another volunteer. As in the Asch experiments, the setup is not what it seems. The learner is actually a member of the research team, well coached in simulating extreme pain, even agony. He is strapped into a chair, replete with formidable-looking wrist electrodes, and given a buzzer he is to press to answer word-choice questions spoken into a microphone by the subject.

The subject and the experimenter sit in another room, observing the learner through a glass partition while the subject manipulates false shock controls. The controls look quite real. They are calibrated with different voltage levels marked by appropriate signs, from "Slight Shock" at 15 volts to "Danger: Severe Shock" at 375-450 volts. A wrong answer or no answer requires the volunteer to give the learner a shock, each successive failure calling for an increase in voltage. At 75 volts, the learner grunts; at 120, he shouts; by 150 he is demanding to be released; by 270 there is agonized screaming and at 330 ominous silence.

How did the subjects—men and women ranging in age from 20 to 50 and including laborers, housewives, engineers and businessmen—respond? Despite screams that pierced the control room, despite the learner's pleas and demands for release, 65 per cent of them obeyed in some trials when the experimenter ordered them to continue the shocks; they kept on administering what they believed were excruciatingly painful doses of electricity to a fellow human being. Here is a sample of the dialogue during one test involving a 50-year-old male subject, who has just administered what he believes to be a 180-volt shock to a protesting learner.

Subject: "I can't stand it. I'm not going to kill that man in there. You hear him hollering?"

Experimenter: "As I told you before, the shocks may be painful but—"

Subject: "But he's hollering. He can't stand it. What's going to happen to him?"

Experimenter: "The experiment requires that you continue."

The subject continues. At 315 volts the groaning learner fails to answer and the subject pleads with him.

Subject: "You got to. You get a shock if you don't answer." The experiment continues, the learner no longer answering and, finally, failing even to groan. At 375 volts, the subject stands up.

Subject: "I think something's happened to that fellow in there. I don't get no answer. He was hollering at less voltage. Can't you check and see if he's all right, please?"

Experimenter: "Not once we've started. Please continue. . . ." It continued to maximum voltage, the subject once seeking and getting assurance that what happened was the experimenter's responsibility.

One female subject who also carried through to the end was a registered nurse. In a post-experiment interview, she was asked if she had thought of stopping despite the orders of the experimenter.

Nurse: "He said, 'Go ahead.' I did. I said to him, 'I don't think I should go on any further.' He said, 'Go on with the experiment.'"

Interviewer: "Is there anything [the learner] could have said that would have caused you to stop the experiment?"

Nurse: "I don't think so."

A male social worker who also went all the way to 450 volts said in retrospect: "What appalled me was that I could possess this capacity for obedience and compliance to a central idea, i.e., the value of a memory experiment, even after it became clear that continued adherence to this value was at the expense of violation of another value, i.e., don't hurt someone else who is helpless and not hurting you. As my wife said, 'You can call yourself Eichmann.'"

The experiments themselves came to be called the Eichmann experiments, after Adolf Eichmann, the Nazi official who justified his role in murdering hundreds of thousands of Jews on the ground that he was only carrying out orders of his superiors. Yet the Eichmann rationalization did not sway all of Milgram's subjects. More than one third held to their individual beliefs and rejected orders they considered improper. An engineer refused to continue when the learner began screaming.

Experimenter: "It is absolutely essential that you continue."

Engineer: "Well I won't—not with the man screaming to get out."

Experimenter: "You have no other choice."

Engineer: "I *do* have a choice. . . . Why don't I have a choice? I came here on my own free will. . . . But if I have to hurt somebody to do that, or if I was in his place, too, I wouldn't stay there. I can't continue. I'm very sorry. I think I've gone too far already, probably."

Later, in an explanation of his action, this man said: "I should have stopped the first time he complained. I did want to stop at that time. I turned around and looked at you. I guess it's a matter of . . . authority. . . . One of the things I think is very cowardly is to try to shove the responsibility onto someone else. See, if I now turned around and said, 'It's your fault . . . not mine,' I would call that cowardly."

Although 35 per cent of the subjects always refused, like the engineer, to bow to authority, the number who yielded was shockingly high; scientists and laymen surveyed before the experiments began had predicted only 1 or 2 per cent of the subjects would carry through to the end. Milgram explains this willing participation of ordinary, humane people in an inhumane exercise as a fundamental, if temporary, personality change: essential traits were altered by the situation. Milgram concludes that when an individual "merges his person into an organizational structure, a new creature replaces autonomous man . . . freed of humane inhibition, mindful only of the sanction of authority." Critics of Milgram's studies—there are many—question his conclusions. They feel the tests prove little unless more is known about differences among the subjects: how many were latent sadists, how many were submissive to begin with.

Ironically, many observers found the gravest issue raised by Milgram's work involves the experiment, not the results. They condemn the way he treated his volunteers. The subjects were never warned that they would be forced to delve into their psyches. Those who behaved like little Eichmanns will live with this self-knowledge for years to come. Criticism of this aspect of Milgram's work has been so strong, inside and outside the scientific community, that his experiments may never be repeated—at least not without major modifications.

An experiment like Milgram's, by virtue of its sensational nature, attracts a degree of attention that is out of proportion to its scientific importance. And yet its results, questioned though they are, seem to buttress those of many less-lurid studies: neither broad labels nor finely analyzed traits nor situations are sufficient to define personality.

Although each personality is at heart enigmatic, the masks people wear are not foolproof. Freud knew they slipped accidentally, with the tongue, to reveal intimate details of character. As psychologists and psychoanalysts have been able to lift these masks, the role of the past (particularly childhood) in determining the present grows clearer.

Psychology also has had some success in predicting future personality development using testing and interviews. These remain imperfect tools, however, which work best when they are used to predict one narrow element of behavior rather than the broad course of individual life style. In recent years, individuals themselves have been openly exploring their own personalities on an unprecedented scale, dropping their masks through such mechanisms as encounter groups and sensitivity-training sessions as they search for understanding of themselves and others. This searching seems to be in response to a widely felt need—in an increasingly dehumanized world—to get in touch with the basics of human character. The late psychologist George A. Kelly viewed all men and women as scientists who tried to organize the evidence of their lives and learn how to construct value systems from that evidence. This current individualistic trend in probing personality, which goes around and beyond scientific institutions like psychotherapy, is a striking example of Kelly's theory in action.

But the individual, alternately being swept along by and battling against the current of his subconscious, and all the while being moved by vast social tides of change, may not always be able to judge his behavior clearly. Other observers—friends, family, scientific or religious counselors—have a different view of his personality. The accuracy of this view, as far as predicting behavior is concerned, varies greatly.

To return to the opening scenario of this chapter, the character called Roger Clendan will appear as many things to many people, depending on how well and long they have been able to observe him in action over life's myriad situations. Those who have to work under Clendan may predict with considerable assurance that between the workday hours of nine to five he is going to be overbearing and irascible, a martinet with few saving graces. A longtime friend from college days, who sees him infrequently, but who always retains a youthful image of him, discerns much more in his character. Clendan, to him, is hot-tempered but loyal, blunt but honest, all-in-all a "good old boy." But the label "martinet" might seem inappropriate to a friend who had never experienced as an underling the sting of Clendan's tongue. Should Clendan ever seek psychological counseling, the counselor over the course of months or years would develop a more complicated picture of the man that would account for his probable behavior in certain situations. The counselor, for example, might unearth certain essential conflicts that make Clendan extremely vulnerable to criticism or to what he sees as challenges to his authority. Given a situation where this vulnerability is tested, his personality will react in a predictable way.

Of all the persons in his life, Mrs. Clendan should be in the best position to judge how her husband will behave. She spends more time with him than any other human being; she has greater opportunity to see the face behind the mask in all the shifting circumstances of a lifetime together. At the beginning of their marriage, she might have been content to generalize about him as "bright . . . ambitious . . . tender." But a young bride's intuitive reading of her husband's personality grows into increasingly complex levels of understanding over the years. Perhaps more than anyone else she will disdain labels to explain his personality, for too often she sees him change with the situation. "He really isn't very smart in handling people . . . he's a perfectionist and drives himself too hard . . . he hides his real emotions to keep from getting hurt." Despite this changeability, certain rhythms in his behavior, certain chords in his disposition recur, and this underlying, unified character forms an enduring image that may be close to the core of her husband's true personality.

Explorers of the psyche

They did not look it, those 48 psychoanalysts who posed for a group photograph in Weimar, Germany, in 1911, but they were revolutionaries—the first men and women to take a truly scientific view of personality. Their leader was Sigmund Freud, the Viennese creator of psychoanalysis whose publications on the hidden, unconscious forces affecting behavior ignited an intellectual revolution.

Though psychoanalysis was developed by physicians specializing in the treatment of neurotics, it also offers a theory of normal personality, a way of explaining how personality develops and influences behavior. Freud and later theorists derived basic ideas by interpreting human actions and hidden feelings in terms of universal attributes —internal conflicts, sexual desires and struggles against authority. All of these had been recognized earlier by novelists and painters, and could be found in the literature and art of many places and periods. Not surprisingly, modern writers and artists have completed the circle, borrowing heavily from the concepts of psychoanalysis and psychology for their works.

These revolutionary ideas were discussed rather amicably at Weimar, and Freud was deferred to as leader. But brilliant disciples such as Carl Jung soon developed divergent theories of their own. Meanwhile, other approaches to personality by men like Gordon Allport, based more on psychology of the normal than on clinical study of neuroses, contributed still other theories. These ideas may contradict one another in some areas, reinforce one another in others, but together offer revealing insights into individual behavior.

At a psychoanalytic congress in Germany in 1911, Freud (beard) and Jung (large bow tie, glasses) are in the second row center.

At 82, Freud works at his London desk just 14 months before his death from cancer.

Freud: sex and conflict

To Freud's original Victorian audience, the real shock in his theory of personality came from his emphasis on sex as the principal force motivating human behavior. As Freud saw it, the natural habitat of sex, aggression and other dark, animal urges was the id, a storehouse of powerful, instinctive impulses. Operating according to Freud's "pleasure principle," the id wants what it wants when it wants it—and goes after it both blindly and ruthlessly.

In Freud's conception, the id is one of three psychological systems comprising the personality. The other two are the superego, a kind of conscience that says no to every socially disapproved pleasure (and sometimes to all pleasures), and the ego, rational arbiter and manager of the personality, which mediates the demands of the primitive id, the constraints of the cruel superego and the exigencies of the real world. Following Freud's "reality principle," a mature ego foregoes present pleasure for future satisfaction.

Freud's view of personality is not cheerful. He saw conflict as inevitable because the needs of id, superego, ego and outside world are inevitably at odds. He believed that man is generally at the mercy of his unconscious, the part of his personality of which he is unaware and which he cannot control. And to Freud's mind, man is not very malleable. Personality, he thought, becomes relatively fixed during the first years of life and is shaped chiefly by immutable biological forces.

Many of Freud's ideas have been contradicted by later work, but his basic framework supports much of the modern understanding of personality. And some notions that he introduced have become essential elements of Western culture, common phrases in everyday speech: sublimation, the expression of socially unacceptable impulses in acceptable ways; the Freudian slip, the seemingly accidental error motivated by an unconscious wish; the Oedipus complex, the small boy's love for mother and hatred of father.

Wish fulfillment, said Freud, is the chief motive for dreaming. In his book "The Interpretation of Dreams," he made his point with a cartoon strip about the dream of a nurse who hears her charge crying to go to the bathroom. Wishing it were unnecessary to get up, the nurse dreams away the problem: she helps the boy relieve himself, and the resultant floods, instead of soaking his bed, serve to float first a kayak, then a gondola, then a sailboat and, ultimately, an ocean liner.

This painting by the French artist Ingres, titled "Oedipus and the Sphinx," illustrates the best-known conflict in Freud's psychoanalytic personality theory, the Oedipus complex. The picture depicts the legendary Greek hero who murdered his father and then married his mother. It was Freud's conviction that what Oedipus did in reality, every small boy does in fantasy. He believed, too, that the child's imaginary deed has profound and lifelong effects on his personality.

Jung: occultism and archetypes

"My successor and crown prince." So Freud called him in 1909. But in 1913 the relationship between Freud and Carl Gustav Jung ended in rancor. One reason was Jung's distaste for Freud's sexual theories. There were other differences between the two psychoanalysts. While the Freudian school holds that major personality changes rarely occur after childhood, the Jungian view is of possibilities for lifelong growth and development.

Another difference lay in the personalities of the men themselves. Freud's temperament led him to take a logical view of personality. But Jung was fascinated by the occult. He believed that alchemy, astrology, Buddhism, certain primitive rituals and religions, mythology and even psychotic hallucinations can shed light on personality and especially on what he called archetypes. These are echoes, he suggested, of man's primordial animal, prehuman and human heritage. Residing in the "collective unconscious," a realm lying even deeper than Freud's unconscious, archetypes, said Jung, are useful because they constitute "the wisdom and experience of uncounted centuries."

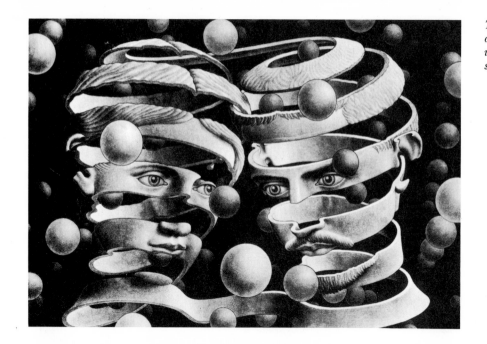

The "Bond of Union," by Dutch graphic artist M. C. Escher, expresses the unity of woman (left) and man (right). Everyone, said Jung, is both female and male.

Shaped in Austria some 25,000 years ago, this statuette suggests Jung's archetype of the ideal mother, an image that is carried in everyone's unconscious.

"The Nightmare," by Swiss romantic painter Henry Fuseli, seems to epitomize what Jung called the shadow, man's passionate, evil and sexual animal nature.

Gordon Allport was graduated from Harvard in 1919, later studied at universities in Berlin, Hamburg and Cambridge, England. He taught psychology at Harvard for nearly 40 years before his death in 1967. An exponent of the trait theory of personality, Allport compiled a list of 17,953 characteristics from Webster's dictionary, among them the smugness personified by the three self-satisfied women in Grant Wood's "Daughters of Revolution" below.

Allport: the 17,953 traits

Psychologist Gordon Allport saw ordinary adults very much as they see themselves, in terms of uncomplicated, readily identifiable characteristics. Personality, he believed, is composed chiefly of traits like honesty, skepticism or kindness—characteristics that Allport thought motivated behavior and made an individual act consistently under many different circumstances.

According to Allport, traits come in three varieties. A "cardinal" trait is a kind of ruling passion that influences virtually everything its possessor says and does. To explain this concept, Allport cited "reverence for life" as the cardinal trait that seemed to govern Dr. Albert Schweitzer's career. Not every personality is ruled by such an all-pervasive sentiment, said Allport, but everyone has perhaps five or 10 central traits that describe his essential nature and explain most of his behavior. In addition, he suggested, everyone has a large number of secondary traits that play a minor role in his personality.

Murray: needs and pressures

Trained in Freudian psychoanalysis, Henry Murray added a number of needs to Freud's list of biological instincts as determinants of individual personality. Among these influences he included the need to play, to understand intellectually, to be autonomous, to accomplish something difficult, to dominate or control other people, and to be deferential to superiors.

Needs, Murray believed, play a major role in shaping human actions, but they are not the only forces that influence personality; quite unlike Freud, Murray gave considerable weight to the total environment as a determinant of behavior. He called environmental influences "press," a word he used to suggest that many factors in the outside world exert pressure on an individual to behave in a particular way. The term is applied to people or to circumstances that are capable of satisfying or frustrating needs.

Thus, he said, the press exerted by a strong rival can get in the way of the need for autonomy. And a new-found friend incorporates a press that is capable of satisfying another need—for affiliation. Said Murray: "The press of an object is what it can do to the subject or for the subject—the power that it has to affect the well-being of the subject in one way or another."

Henry Murray's theory that personality is determined by the interaction of internal needs and external pressures is epitomized by William Blake's engraving "Urizen Sunk in the Waters of Materialism." If the struggling figure of the godlike Urizen is taken to represent human needs, the surrounding waters might then be interpreted as one of the environmental stresses that frequently prevent a person from reaching the goals that he cherishes most in life.

Rogers: the real self vs. the ideal

At the heart of Carl Rogers' theory is his belief that every individual can shape his own personality. He held that the person who would like to be different must first acknowledge his "self" as it is—appraise his own personality candidly without either denying his weaknesses or condemning himself too harshly for them. The next step requires conscious effort to try to become the "ideal self," the kind of person that the individual would like to be.

To sum up this two-part process, Rogers once wrote that "Self-acceptance is the beginning of change." To illustrate his point, he described a successful engineer who first managed to see that he was cold and aloof to his family and associates and only then succeeded in developing an affectionate understanding of his wife and son.

Rogers knew that self-realization is harder than his example makes it seem. One problem, he pointed out, is the natural tendency to make the personality fit other people's values instead of the individual's own. In addition, a person may too readily accept another's judgment about him: for instance, he may believe he is bad, weak or incompetent just because someone tells him so. Rogers has suggested that the successful person is one who has confidence in his own judgment and a profound distrust for everything that is not borne out by his own experience.

Carl Rogers first studied for the ministry, then turned to child-guidance work, subsequently began to teach, and finally became a psychotherapist and author.

Half naked, half clothed, Picasso's 1932 portrayal of a "Girl before a Mirror" suggests the twin images of Carl Rogers' ideal and actual selves.

Pablo Picasso *Girl before a Mirror.* 1932. The Museum of Modern Art, New York.

A magnificent view or a joyous love can often trigger a "peak experience," Maslow thought. Chagall celebrated both in his "St. Jean Cap Ferrat."

Maslow: peaks of experience

Among personality theorists, Abraham Maslow was perhaps the most optimistic. He chided Freud for his view of the unconscious as little more than a source of potentially destructive impulses; to Maslow, the unconscious was the fountainhead "of creativeness, of joy, of happiness, of goodness." It contained, he thought, not only powerful drives that must be tamed but also equally powerful "metaneeds," impulses that cause human beings to seek justice, truth and wholeness.

Far more than most psychologists, Maslow believed deeply in man's capacity for fulfillment. "In practically every human being," he asserted, "there is an active will toward health, an impulse toward growth, or toward the actualization of human potentialities."

Among these potentialities are what Maslow called "peak experiences," the idea for which he is probably best known. These are not moments of ordinary happiness, but heights of transcendent ecstasy in which perceptions sharpen and awareness of time and space dim. Music and religion, natural childbirth or sex may stimulate such exaltation. "Love for the body," Maslow wrote, "awareness of the body and a reverence for the body—these are good paths to peak experiences."

Sullivan: people shape people

Harry Stack Sullivan, who died in 1949, was an expert on schizophrenia known for the technique he developed to treat his patients in face-to-face interviews.

Human relations play the key role in Harry Stack Sullivan's "interpersonal" theory of personality. He held that an individual is shaped chiefly by the nature of his relationships with others, beginning at birth, continuing throughout life and including not only actual dealings with others but also relationships that are remembered from times past, imagined during waking hours, fantasied in dreams at night and even fabricated in hallucinations.

If human interactions are rewarding, Sullivan maintained, personality develops favorably; if they are upsetting, it may become disturbed or distorted. In fact, said Sullivan, fear of social disapproval has a greater impact than some of the influences Freud identified, such as tensions arising from unsatisfied physical needs.

Interacting guests in John Koch's painting "The Cocktail Party" illustrate Sullivan's idea of personality as the product of relationships.

Attributed to Giorgione, "The Three Ages of Man" suggests Erikson's theory of change.

Erikson: eight critical stages

Psychoanalyst Erik H. Erikson believes that a normal human goes through eight stages of personality development. In each period, from infancy through maturity to old age, the individual faces a specific crisis; if all goes well, he emerges with some aspect of his personality more fully developed than before.

During infancy, for example, Erikson sees a crisis centering around confidence. Only when a baby's physical and emotional needs are sensitively filled does he develop basic trust, a feeling that the world is a good place to live in and that he can rely on himself and on other people.

Most familiar of Erikson's critical problems is the identity crisis of the adolescent stage: the young person's difficulty in recognizing all the unique qualities that make him an individual and in understanding how these qualities ought to be developed. To use Erikson's own example, he is like Biff in Arthur Miller's play *Death of a Salesman:* "I just can't take hold, Mom, I can't take hold of some kind of a life." But the youth who meets his identity crisis successfully emerges with a sense of wholeness and continuity.

Erik Erikson studied in Vienna under Freud's daughter Anna before moving to the U.S.

Change through Time

6

In the autumn of 1889 a Polish-born naval officer named Jozef Teodor Konrad Korzeniowski, veteran of 11 years in the British merchant marine, was temporarily without a vessel and was living in a flat in London. One morning after breakfast, without forethought, Korzeniowski sat down at a desk and began writing. He wrote about a man he had met a year before while sailing as a second mate on the steamship *Vidar*, gathering rubber and cane in Borneo and the Celebese Islands.

"Till I began to write that novel," Korzeniowski later recalled, "I had written nothing but letters, and not very many of these. I never made a note of a fact, of an impression or of an anecdote in my life." He had been a hard-working and expert mariner, had earned his captain's license and had given every sign of devotion to the sea.

The novel that Captain Korzeniowski began in his London flat turned out to be *Almayer's Folly*. It was the first published work of an author who went on to produce such classics as *Lord Jim, Youth* and *Typhoon* under the Anglicized version of his name: Joseph Conrad. At age 37 this apparently contented mariner suddenly left the sea for good and became a man of letters. More amazing, he wrote in his acquired language, English, rather than his native Polish. Why a man raised in Poland, at home on a ship's bridge rather than behind a writing desk, should suddenly emerge as a full-blown English author is one of the fascinating enigmas of literary history—and of individual behavior.

Conrad's dramatic turnabout illustrates a truth about human nature: individuals change. Not everyone throws over one career and embarks on a completely different one, as Conrad did, but all people do change at least to some degree as they grow older. It could hardly be otherwise. As the years pass, each individual encounters experiences that are bound to modify his ways of seeing himself and his reactions to the world around him. He is shaped in part by the passage of time, just as he is shaped in infancy by the way his parents bring him up. Even such basic qualities as intellectual gifts, creative abilities and personality structure appear to undergo alterations, although radical change seems rare.

This growth and change proceeds from within a person, shaped by external influences but not necessarily ordained by them. Each individual reacts in his own private way to the circumstances he encounters—for every mariner who became a novelist, there have been thousands who found fulfillment in the sea itself. Yet there is also a different kind of alteration of behavior, one that is specifically and deliberately ordered by forces outside the individual. He cannot choose—consciously or unconsciously—how he will respond. The desired response is spelled out for him, and his only choice is to comply, altering his behavior in the specified way, or to resist—perhaps at considerable risk.

Deliberate attempts to shape behavior are ancient and ubiquitous. Anybody who has undergone military training knows that it demands behavior changes in the individual. Schools also set about to alter—for the better, it is hoped—the behavior of the child. Advertising is intended to influence people's buying habits, and in doing so it may alter what they eat and where, how they sleep, even how they react to friends and family.

Today, much has been learned about the mechanisms underlying such deliberately induced behavior change. And this new knowledge has led to more efficient behavior manipulation with special techniques that are finding wide use—and arousing even wider controversy. Their proponents praise these procedures for their apparent effectiveness in education, medicine and the rehabilitation of criminals. To their critics, some of the methods that have been used to alter the behavior of people are inhumane tools for thought control that already have produced evil results and that threaten greater harm in the future.

I n all probability, most human change up to the present has been elicited from within the individual rather than forced on him from outside. Conrad is a good example, but he was far from being the only person to make a major shift in career and life style in the middle years. Another was the French painter Paul Gauguin. As a young man of 23, Gauguin went to work as a stockbroker for Bertin and Company, an old, staid Parisian financial house. He proved to be a talented and successful broker and, with a good income assured, he married a respectable bourgeoise woman. They started a family that eventually included five children.

But driven by some inner impulse, the good businessman and husband began to paint on weekends. At first his wife approved—it was healthy for a man to have a hobby. Then Gauguin began associating with the avant-garde painters of the day, the Impressionists, who, like the avant-garde in any era, struck respectable people as uncouth. His wife's alarm turned to panic when suddenly, at age 35, Gauguin realized that painting was his life and abruptly resigned from his job. Seeing their son-in-law give up a secure and lucrative career for anything as disreputable as art profoundly shocked his wife's respectable family. Gauguin abandoned his wife and children and eventually, as everyone knows, fled all bourgeois trappings to live and paint in Tahiti.

Similar artistic conversions—abrupt breaks in the middle years—have been known to operate in reverse. Arthur Rimbaud, who revolutionized French poetry in the 19th Century when still in his teens, abruptly abandoned his writing career at 19 and became a traveling salesman who occasionally smuggled guns to Ethiopian tribes as a sideline. Herman Melville, disillusioned by the commercial failure of *Moby Dick* and other novels, gave up writing to be a clerk in New York's customhouse.

Abrupt changes of life are by no means a monopoly of famous artists and writers. Increasingly today, ordinary people, bored or disillusioned with their careers, are quitting and starting entirely new lives. Newspapers carry frequent stories about salesmen who become priests and, conversely, priests who leave holy orders, take jobs and get married—often to former nuns. An economics professor may become an opera singer. Bankers return to the soil as farmers, and housewives leave home and become executives. This sort of career switching seems to have a special appeal in the United States. One survey, conducted in 1972, found that 49 per cent of a group of 2,700 successful businessmen had either considered changing their occupations or had actually done so in the previous five years. An educational program designed to aid career switchers is offered at the Stony Brook campus of the State University of New York. And career changers in California founded a club, mockingly named the Black Bart Brigade after a 19th Century Californian who made a notable change in life style—from honest prospector to stagecoach robber.

Career shifting may, of course, be caused by circumstance, but it may also proceed from a deeply felt shift in internal priorities. The possibility of significant change was recognized even by Freud, who believed that fundamental patterns of behavior were largely fixed by biological forces and infant experience, and therefore could be altered only by heroic measures. Most authorities today are more optimistic. They see behavior changing in several ways. There could be a rearrangement in the mixture of characteristics making up an individual's personality, so that his overall behavior pattern shifted. Or certain qualities, always present but hidden, might be released; that is, existing potential might be realized.

In such cases, how much change takes place depends on the strength of the forces influencing change. Of course, no one expects to inject intelligence into a dullard and convert him into a genius. But there is plenty of evidence that even such a fundamental characteristic as intelligence may grow or diminish as an individual passes through life.

For some years it seemed that intellectual capacity decreased steadily as a person aged. When the first studies were made, starting in the early 1920s, a consistent pattern emerged. An intelligence peak was reached between the ages of 19 and 21 with a distinct decline through the middle and later years. The scores of more than 15,000 officers who took the U.S. Army's Alpha intelligence test *(page 75)* in World War I showed those under 20 averaging 150, those between 25 and 30 scoring 143 and the 50 to 60 group dropping to 120.

But the Alpha test was made up of a number of subtests, and when psychologists analyzed the scores on each of these rather than the overall results, an interesting pattern appeared. The studies showed that there had been no decline on the information and vocabulary subtests until age 60. Still further analysis showed, in fact, that people improved in these areas as time went on—humans do not forget all they know as time passes but rather absorb further information. Older people did not do quite so well as 20-year-olds in the parts of the test demanding speed in solving new problems; mental agility seems to decline with passing time. But the overall intelligence of older people holds its own.

These findings were confirmed by psychologist W. A. Owens, one of the few men to persevere in a longitudinal study of intelligence—that is, in repeated examinations of the same people. Owens' subjects, tested several times over a span of 42 years, from 1919 to 1961, showed gains in nearly all of the Alpha's subtests, even after they had reached their sixties. In some respects, his results showed the same pattern as the other Alpha studies: the greatest gain was in the informational and verbal subtests, the least gain (or in some cases a slight loss) occurred in the sections demanding speedy problem solving.

Still other studies of maturing intelligence have turned up what may be a more significant fact: people who remain mentally active—involved and interested in the life around them—preserve their mental acuity longer than inactive people. It would appear that the improvement or deterioration of the intellectual faculties is up to the individual himself.

If intelligence changes in quality—and sometimes even in quantity —what of creativity? Whether people change in this subtle, hard-to-study area remains a question. It seems clear from the evidence of many creative lives—such as the thousands of outstanding individuals studied by H. C. Lehman *(page 93)*—that this characteristic generally shows itself early: most scientists and artists do their best work in their twenties and thirties. It also seems evident that most children have the capacity to be creative; under the guidance of gifted teachers, many paint imaginative pictures and write evocative poetry. Children have an eagerness to try anything that seems to open the wellsprings of creativity. Perhaps the reason many adults are not notably creative is that they lose this childhood spark as they grow older and are forced to face life's hard realities. And perhaps part of the secret of why some adults—especially younger ones—do create is that they retain some of the ebullience and willingness to take risks characteristic of children. If creativity changes, it would appear to decrease with age. Even such a fountain of creativity as Picasso, who continued to produce great works throughout his long life, did his most daring and innovative work in his earlier years. Coleridge's best poetry was a product of his twenties and early thirties. But then there are the examples of Conrad and Gauguin, whose creative urges were liberated in mid-life, or of the wonderful American primitive painter Grandma Moses, who started her career in art in her seventies. Perhaps the safest generalization that can be made about creativity is that it may flower late—and even persist into old age, as it did with Leonardo—but that normally it shows itself early and later may drop off, at least in originality. This conclusion was

Effecting a dramatic career change, Joseph Conrad (top row, center) switched from seafaring to become a great novelist.

buttressed by a study by Wayne Dennis of Brooklyn College, of scholars, scientists and artists who lived to be 80. Dennis' results suggest that peaks of creativity may be more likely in early years, but creative people remain creative on a more modest level all their lives.

Human personality is perhaps even harder to analyze than creativity. The total personality is made up of many elements, ranging from the deepest unconscious drives to the changeable public face that each person contrives to present to the world. Some ingrained aspects of the personality seem immutable. A person with a deeply implanted distrust of other people, perhaps the product of cruel childhood experiences, may be condemned to carry this fear all his life although possibly it can be removed by lengthy psychoanalysis. Or a naturally happy and confident person may preserve an optimistic outlook through severe trials. A study of 90 people who underwent the terrible persecutions of Nazi Germany found that they had preserved their basic personality structures to a remarkable degree. There was, the study said, an "extraordinary continuity and sameness of individual personalities. . . . An optimistic, extroverted, affable advertising man is ruined by the Nazis, but eventually turns up in South America as an optimistic, extroverted, affable advertising man." Such persistence of personality doubtless owed a great deal to willed resistance to change. Apparently people struggle to maintain essential values that they prize, even when outside forces exert tremendous pressure to change.

The first long-range study of personality, begun in 1929 by the Fels Institute of Yellow Springs, Ohio, seems to support this idea. Researchers started keeping tabs on 89 infants. Personality assessments were made at intervals from birth to three years, from three to six, from six to 10 and so on. In 1957, the 71 subjects still in the study were assessed in their midtwenties. Marked similarities were found between child and adult. Aggressive boys had become aggressive men, cheerful and competent girls were still bright and able. The study confirmed what most people feel, that neither they themselves nor their friends change much in essential ways, that for most there is a continuity that makes the total person recognizable at 10, at 20 and at 50.

If people's fundamental natures resist easy change, less deeply implanted personality characteristics do appear to alter through experience and the passage of time. The individual adapts his qualities to his circumstance, suppressing disadvantageous ones, strengthening advantageous ones. Rarely does the aggressive boy become meek in later life; he is likely, however, to learn to temper his aggressiveness. This sort of evolutionary development of personality is documented in an ambitious, long-range study by Jack Block of the University of California.

Block began by testing and interviewing a group of 171 boys and girls when they were in their early teens. He then evaluated them when they were in their late teens and once more when they were in their thirties. He found considerable personality adaptation, especially among the 30-year-olds. Out in the world, when most of them were married and responsible for children, Block's subjects were no longer quite the same people they had been in their youth. The men, Block reports in his book *Lives Through Time*, were generally "more dependable, more productive, more satisfied with self, more clear-cut and consistent in their personalities." But these improvements had been gained at some cost, since the men were also less responsive—to humor, to beauty, to other people. Many of the women changed in comparable but not identical ways, becoming more responsible, more affectionate, and generally more outgoing in nature.

Those changes were relatively minor, and were presumably brought about by circumstance. In addition, people can change their personalities drastically if they desire to do so strongly enough. The most potent tool in this process is Freud's great discovery, psychoanalysis.

People who are neurotically shy, for example, or who helplessly repeat behavior patterns that disturb the normal functioning of their lives, can sometimes restructure their personalities through the process of analysis. A great deal has been written about psychoanalysis that makes it sound complex and arcane. Its essence, however, is simple and logical: the analyst tries to help the person locate those experiences in the past, often in childhood, that produced the crippling personality quirk. He does this, first of all, by inviting the person being analyzed to talk aimlessly about his thoughts and memories, skipping from subject to subject without restraint, no matter how trivial the matter may seem or how odd and embarrassing it may be. Over many sessions of such free association—perhaps three a week over several years—the subject becomes able to reach further and further into the dark recesses of his unconscious and finds himself expressing previously blocked emotions that surrounded upsetting —traumatic—experiences. As the patient talks, the analyst listens intently for telltale repetitions of words or ideas (or for obvious gaps in the narration) that may indicate still suppressed experiences or emotions. Many of Freud's followers also ask the subject to describe his dreams: dreams, Freud discovered, often contain hints of troublesome material so deeply imbedded in the unconscious and so unbearable to remember that the conscious mind is powerless to bring it to the surface. The analyst fits this material together as it surfaces, locating and isolating past experiences that have resulted in the subject's present behavior. In effect he helps the patient to relive his past and understand the motivations that up to now have been unconscious; the understanding can free him from his guilts and repressions, with resulting beneficial changes in personality.

The most famous example of a personality transformed by psychoanalysis is one of Freud's own cases, an 18-year-old girl he called Dora. She was a roiling mass of hatred and despair who felt hostile toward her father, had always despised her mother, did not speak to her brother and avoided seeing her friends. She was chronically tired and could seldom muster the concentration to work. She had threatened suicide. She was tormented by the knowledge that her father was having an af-

One of history's most dramatic life-style changes was effected by the celebrated French artist Paul Gauguin (right), who, in 1883, gave up a successful career on the Bourse (far right), Paris' stock exchange, to be a full-time painter. He left his family and in 1891, at age 42 (below), sailed for Tahiti. There, living in a thatch-roofed hut with a Tahitian mistress, he produced masterful canvases like the one shown at right, below.

fair with the wife of a family friend, Frau K, but Dora also suffered from a galaxy of physical ailments—coughing, appendicitis pains and an inability to speak—which suggested to Freud how he might enable her to regain a normal personality.

Freud searched Dora's past for experiences that might explain her hostilities and despair. Under his gentle prodding, she began to recall painful memories she had forced into her unconscious. A couple of years earlier, it turned out, she had been kissed by Herr K, husband of her father's mistress. Dora was outraged and ran away but said nothing to anyone. Later, Herr K propositioned her and she slapped him—but waited two weeks before informing her father of the incident. When she finally told him, he made light of the matter, but his reassurance unsettled her more. She came to suspect that her father and Herr K had made a deal: Herr K would make no trouble about her father's affair with his wife in return for permission to seduce Dora.

The resulting distrust and even hatred of her father warred in Dora's mind with her previous adoration of him. Freud concluded that the physical ills and the suicide note were, in large part, unconscious devices designed by Dora to woo her father away from Frau K, and to regain his love for herself.

As the analysis progressed, Freud discovered that Dora's obsession with her father's love affair was in large measure a smokescreen hiding two even more painful repressed thoughts: Dora's unacknowledged and deeply suppressed love for Herr K, who—despite the slap—she wished had seduced her, and an even more deeply repressed homosexual attraction to Frau K. Three salient pieces of evidence pointed to Dora's suppressed love for Herr K. She had waited two weeks to tell her father of the kiss; unconsciously, she had been waiting for Herr K to make another advance. The coughing attacks and periods of being unable to speak came only when Herr K was away on business trips; Dora then had no need to talk. The abdominal pains of her false appendicitis had occurred exactly nine months after Herr K's kiss; she had, unconsciously again, wished she was pregnant and had staged a close imitation of labor pains.

With these and other deductions, Freud managed to make Dora understand her buried love for Herr K, her love-hate relationship with her father and her complex jealousies—of her father's attachment to Frau K, of Frau K herself and of Herr K. But after only 11 weeks of treatment, Dora broke off the analysis and Freud could do no more.

Even this truncated analysis altered Dora's personality. Her physical symptoms virtually disappeared, she threw off her fascination with Herr K and her exaggerated love for her father, she went back to work, eventually married an engineer and lived a satisfactory life. As Freud summed it up, she "had been reclaimed once more by the realities of life."

Changes such as Block and Freud demonstrated, arising from within the individual, may be unconscious responses to the pressures of life or intentional efforts to meet a deep personal need. But because they are personal, they are quite different from the second type of change, alterations in behavior deliberately and specifically ordered by outside agencies. In its simplest form, such deliberate manipulation is nothing but training. The Roman military establishment knew how to take an individual peasant youth and remold him into the standardized legionaire. Close-order drill, common in military training then as today, is a form of behavior manipulation. The individual is forced to respond immediately and automatically to commands, a process that ingrains the instant obedience necessary on a battlefield. Every child, for that matter, undergoes a kind of behavior alteration as it grows and adapts to society. It is trained by its parents to control its original anarchic little ego and be socialized. Most of these changes in behavior, whether of an infant or a soldier, are induced by a system of rewards for desired behavior and punishments for undesired behavior, although sometimes only one or the other is used.

The ancient technique of the carrot and the stick has been greatly refined by 20th Century research, leading to the development of processes technically known as conditioning but often called behavior modification. Like older schemes, behavior modification depends on rewards or punishments or both, but it can produce startling changes in behavior, and startlingly fast. Its principles lie behind the teaching machines used in many schools, and it has been applied directly to rid people of phobias and undesirable habits, to relieve sexual deviants of their abnormal desires, even to treat patients with such serious mental illnesses as schizophrenia.

Even these seemingly admirable uses of behavior modification are the source of some controversy; they draw fire from those who object to any attempt to force people into a particular way of behaving. But far stronger attacks on conditioning are aimed at some other applications, particularly its use on prisoners—criminal or political. In some prisons in the United States, attempts to reform criminals employ conditioning punishments that seem perilously close to torture. More plainly evil is the way conditioning techniques seem to have been involved in thought control. The brainwashing conducted in past decades in Russia and China, ostensibly intended to reform enemies of the state, apparently stems from principles of conditioning, and this use in recent times is cause enough for genuine concern about future misuse by other authoritarian governments.

The passions stimulated by the new methods of behavior modification are not so strongly directed at older and simpler forms of manipulation. Perhaps the reason is that they *are* older and milder, and they have become more or less accepted. Advertising, for example, though occasionally criticized for some of its alterations of the way people act, is also recognized as an essential force in modern economic life.

Perhaps the advertising campaign most widely credited with influencing a change in behavior was launched in the 1920s by the makers of a popular brand of cigarettes. Women had just begun to smoke; the cigarette manufacturer wanted to encourage this trend and increase sales. But at first, fear of adverse public reaction prevented the company from showing

Self-change self-taught

If you are feeling stupid, haven't had a creative idea in years, or think your personality is repellent, don't despair. There is something you can do about it. Read a book. At least that is what the books claim, promising to show any reader how to change himself into the kind of person he wants to be.

Such volumes, with advice on everything from increasing intelligence to promoting creativity, are among the most popular forms of reading. One Japanese treatise on sharpening the wits, *Calisthenics for Your Brains* by Akiro Tago, sold 4.5 million copies. In the United States, a book that promised to instill the confidence necessary for worldly success, Dr. Norman Vincent Peale's *The Power of Positive Thinking*, has sold over three million copies.

But the self-help books with widest appeal are those aimed at helping the individual make over his personality. The champion of the genre is Dale Carnegie's *How To Win Friends and Influence People*. First published in 1936, this mixture of common-sense advice and homely anecdotes *(excerpted below)* has sold over 12 million copies and has appeared in over 30 languages.

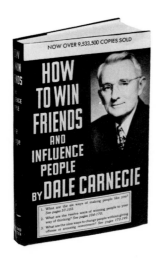

Yes, you who are reading these lines possess powers of various sorts which you habitually fail to use; and one of these powers which you are probably not using to the fullest extent is your magic ability to praise people and inspire them with a realization of their latent possibilities.

The average man is more interested in his own name than he is in all the other names on earth put together. Remember that name and call it easily, and you have paid him a subtle and very effective compliment. But forget it or misspell it—and you have placed yourself at a sharp disadvantage.

The unvarnished truth is that almost every man you meet feels himself superior to you in some way; and a sure way to his heart is to let him realize in some subtle way that you recognize his importance in his little world.

There is only one way under high heaven to get the best of an argument—and that is to avoid it. You may be right, dead right, as you speed along in your argument; but as far as changing the other man's mind is concerned, you will probably be just as futile as if you were wrong.

Actions speak louder than words, and a smile says, "I like you. You make me happy. I am glad to see you."
That is why dogs make such a hit. They are so glad to see us that they almost jump out of their skins. So, naturally, we are glad to see them.
An insincere grin? No. That doesn't fool anybody. We know it is mechanical and we resent it. I am talking about a real smile, a heartwarming smile, a smile that comes from within, the kind of a smile that will bring a good price in the market place.

a woman actually smoking. Instead, a slim, elegantly gowned woman—whom many less-beautiful women no doubt would have liked to resemble—was shown asking her impeccably dressed cigarette-smoking beau to "Blow the smoke my way." Heartened by the success of this ad, the cigarette maker then tried an approach calculated to reach weight-conscious women, encouraging them to reach for a smoke instead of a sweet. No one can tell whether this advertising campaign was indeed responsible for spreading the smoking habit so widely among women, but most observers believe it played a significant role in making the cigarette-smoking woman socially acceptable.

The technique of image-building used in the cigarette campaign—that slim, elegant women enjoy cigarette smoke—has been augmented since World War II by motivational research. Advertising agencies have employed teams of psychologists to help them manipulate people's guilts, snobberies, secret desires, anxieties and feelings of inadequacy, and to assist in the design of images that are associated in people's minds with rewards or punishments.

Two famous advertisements of the 1950s played on snob appeal, promising purchasers of the advertised products the reward of enhanced suavity. One showed an aristocratic gentleman with a black eye patch wearing the advertiser's brand of shirt. Not only was the model an obvious aristocrat, but also he was usually shown indulging in some fashionable hobby, such as collecting valuable ship models. The second snob-appeal image implied that the drinker of one brand of quinine water would be rewarded by association with the rugged, worldly look of an ex-officer in the British Navy.

Other advertisements, playing on people's guilts and anxieties, threaten punishment if their product is ignored. This is generally the message of soap ads—the housewife's laundry will be gray with unremoved grime, and she will be sneered at by her neighbors unless she employs this or that washday detergent. In like fashion, most deodorant advertising is aimed at the fear of being socially offensive. Concern about bad breath has similarly been fostered by mouthwash manufacturers.

The behavior altered by advertising is often trivial—an individual is pressed to buy one brand of something over another. The newer techniques of conditioning bring about more serious transformations of human behavior. Most of these efforts stem from laboratory research that began early in this century.

The first scientist to experiment with methods of modifying behavior was a Russian physiologist named Ivan Pavlov. He placed a tube in a dog's salivary gland, then presented the dog with food and measured the amount of saliva produced as a natural reflex when the hungry dog sighted the food. He next rigged up a light that would flash just before he put food in the dog's dish. Soon the dog began to salivate when the light went on, and continued to do so even when food did not follow—the salivation reflex was triggered by the light rather than by food. Pavlov also experimented with reflexes to pain. He gave a dog's hind paw an electric shock. The dog, of course, lifted its paw. Then he accompanied each shock with a noise, the sounding of a tuning fork. Soon the dog was lifting its paw every time it heard the tuning fork; once again a new reflex had been introduced in the dog's behavior pattern.

Pavlov called these responses conditioned reflexes, because he had conditioned the dog to respond reflexively to an artificial stimulus, such as the light or the tuning fork, instead of the natural stimulus of food or pain. But the ability to condition a reflex was only the first step. The reverse procedure later turned out to be equally significant. Pavlov found that he could *de*condition his dogs; by stopping use of the artificial stimulus he could make the dog stop associating it with the natural stimulus. Eventually he discovered that he could instill and then replace many different kinds of reflex actions almost at will.

Pavlov's experiments have been extended by many investigators to make conditioning apply not only to the automatic, mindless actions of reflexes but also to learned behavior that is controlled by the conscious brain. Much of the work in this field has been done by B. F. Skinner of Harvard. Putting rats and pigeons in "Skinner Boxes," he has taught them a variety of behaviors by a technique called reinforcement. The rat presses a lever inside the box and a pellet of food rolls into a cup. The rat soon learns that lever-pressing means food. (Skinner uses only rewards in conditioning, but other experimenters achieve similar results with so-called negative reinforcement—i.e., punishment.)

Such conditioning techniques can be used on man to change his behavior. Some alcoholics, for example, have been cured of their addiction by a system that rewards them for reducing their consumption of liquor. It is also apparent how these behavior-changing techniques could be used to regiment people's behavior by brainwashing—deconditioning and reconditioning an individual, much as Pavlov did dogs, to remove previous habits and thoughts and replace them with new ideas.

The world first saw brainwashing in action in the 1930s in Russia, although few people at that time fully understood what was going on. Stalin had jailed numbers of Red Army officers and Communist Party officials, whom he evidently feared as threats to his power, accusing them of crimes against the Soviet state. As the trials of these men went on, one after another admitted that he had in fact committed crimes against his country. Many of the statements were absurd; these men could not have done the deeds they confessed to. Many were known to have been faithful government servants. Observers assumed that confessions had been forced from them by torture. But in court the men did not appear to have been beaten or in poor physical shape. Furthermore, some of the men confessed almost cheerfully, as if they were getting a great weight off their minds.

The answer to this mystery slowly filtered out of Russia after World War II. It seems that the victims of the "purge trials" had been so effectively brainwashed that they really had come to believe their own confessions. The technique used was not primarily physical torture, although that was employed. The principal mechanism was mental torture, a systematic deconditioning or confusion of all that the accused men knew, an unhinging of the normal processes of the mind through endless interrogations by relentless questioners. The interrogators, having induced this mental confusion, had then suggested to the men's fuddled brains the treasons they were required to confess. In their mental agony, the prisoners could no longer remember what they had done and what they had not —and so they could not defend themselves against spurious suggestions concerning their "crimes." Ultimately they collapsed and agreed that they had committed the crimes ascribed to them.

Brainwashing along similar lines was used by the Chinese on American prisoners during the Korean War. The Chinese pressed certain prisoners, especially pilots, to confess to war crimes such as dropping germ-laden bombs. They also wanted prisoners to accept Communist ideology. A number of prisoners did both.

The Chinese used several techniques to achieve this result. Physical torture was rare, but extreme discomfort was induced by keeping the men in cold, cramped cells and feeding them bad food. The prisoners were also degraded by preventing them from making any attempt at personal hygiene. More insidious, however, was the mental torture. As in Russia in the 1930s, the prisoners were interrogated relentlessly. Every value they possessed was condemned. In an effort to induce guilt, the interrogators insisted that the prisoners' professions of belief were false and hypocritical as well as foolish. The men were subjected to interminable Chinese propaganda, but news from the outside world was blocked. When the interrogators were not at work, the prisoners were locked up with Chinese cell mates who continued to mock and revile them and also prevented them from sleeping. This treatment was intended to confuse—and ultimately destroy—the prisoner's self-image, to decondition his sense of identity and integrity, and to undermine his basic values. In effect, it caused an identity crisis. Then the Chinese captors suggested to the prisoners new values and beliefs with which they might construct new identities, and offered them a way out of the guilt they had been made to feel: confession. The captors, having weakened all of the prisoners' defense mechanisms, then promised kinder treatment, the privilege of washing, more comfortable cells and so on. It is no wonder that under such circumstances a number of the prisoners gave in.

The mystery, in fact, is why so many were able to resist the pressures. Interviewed after the war had ended, many ex-prisoners who had staved off brainwashing attributed their power to hold out to faith. They did not necessarily mean religious belief, although that was sometimes a factor, but rather faith in their native country, friends and parents—most of all faith that they would survive and eventually return home. They somehow held their identities intact by keeping in the forefront of their minds the things that had formed their individualities. They refused to allow the extreme pressure of the deconditioning to destroy their faith in themselves.

The extremes to which brainwashing might be carried are described in George Orwell's novel *1984*. In this book the state uses behavior modification to coerce its own citizens to conform. One of Orwell's characters, Winston Smith, tries to assert his individual love of freedom but is arrested and later, wired into an electroshock machine, is questioned by the interrogator, O'Brien. O'Brien says:

" 'You preferred to be a lunatic, a minority of one. . . . You believe that reality is something objective, external, existing in its own right. . . . But I tell you, Winston, that reality is not external. Reality exists in the human mind and nowhere else. Not in the individual mind which can make mistakes, and in any case soon perishes; only in the mind of the Party, which is collective and immortal. Whatever the Party holds to be the truth *is* the truth. . . . Do you remember writing in your diary, "Freedom is the freedom to say that two plus two make four"?'

'Yes,' said Winston.

O'Brien held up his left hand, its back toward Winston, with the thumb hidden and the four fingers extended.

'How many fingers am I holding up, Winston?'

'Four.'

'And if the Party says that it is not four but five—then how many?'

'Four.'

The word ended in a gasp of pain. The needle of the dial had shot up to fifty-five. The sweat had sprung out all over Winston's body. The air tore into his lungs and issued again in deep groans."

As Winston persists in saying, "Four," the shocks increase in intensity. Winston finally cries out, "Five!" but that is not enough to stop the shocks. This behavior modification requires not a lying response to end the pain but a total surrender of the mind. And, at last, Winston surrenders to O'Brien's demands.

" 'How many fingers am I holding up, Winston?'

'I don't know. I don't know. You will kill me if you do that again. Four, five, six—in all honesty I don't know.'

'Better,' said O'Brien."

The uses to which the techniques of behavioral conditioning have occasionally been put—and the potential imagined by such authors as Orwell in *1984* and Anthony Burgess in *Clockwork Orange*—are understandably frightening. Conditioning, like many important discoveries, can be used either for good or for evil. Sometimes the good and the evil seem almost inextricably mixed. This would seem to be the case with a long-term experiment in behavior modification in the Maryland prison system.

Maryland's Patuxent Institution for Defective Delinquents started using behavior conditioning techniques in 1955. The staff included an ample number of psychologists, psychiatrists and social workers, and they regarded Patuxent more as a therapeutic community than a prison, despite

High priest of directed behavior

Harvard psychologist B. F. Skinner, a leading advocate of behavior modification, developed many of the techniques of operant conditioning. He taught pigeons to play table tennis by rewarding them with some grain for every right move, and he believes that similar conditioning can produce any desired behavior pattern in human beings.

Skinner employs only rewards to condition behavior. He believes that punishment breeds hostility and that "a person who has been punished is not less inclined to behave in a given way; at best, he learns how to avoid punishment." Behaviorists who disagree use electric shocks or other punishments, sometimes in conjunction with rewards, in treating homosexuality, alcoholism and a multitude of neurotic symptoms.

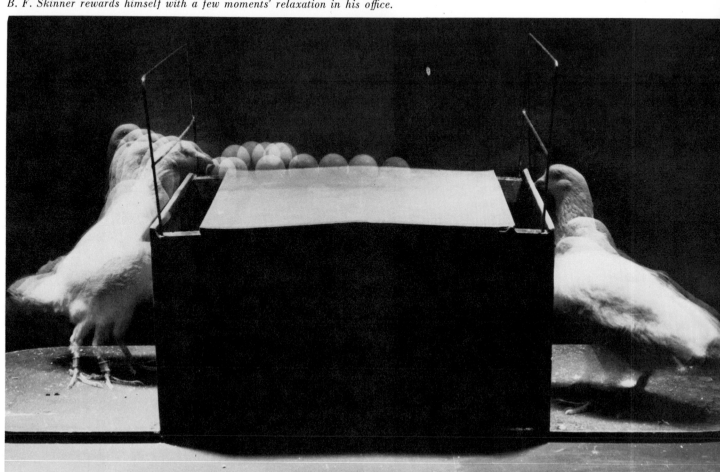

B. F. Skinner rewards himself with a few moments' relaxation in his office.

Pigeons, conditioned by Skinner to play a kind of table tennis, shove a ball with their beaks to try to push it past each other into slots.

its barbed-wire fences and armed guards. The institution's aim was to change the antisocial attitudes of the inmates, most of whom had been convicted of violent crimes.

Patuxent used both positive and negative reinforcement. Good behavior brought privileges and hope of early release, rewards that were supposed to reinforce desirable habits as they were learned. Bad behavior brought punishment, loss of privileges and deferred the day of release. There was a four-tiered status system based on how a prisoner performed in Patuxent's vocational and group psychotherapy programs, and on how he responded to discipline. Second-level prisoners, for example, were required to be in bed by 11. Third levelers went to bed at 11:30 and those in the top level could stay up as late as they chose. Only table tennis was available at the third level but the fourth had pool tables as well. And only prisoners of the fourth level could have Sunday afternoon picnics with their families. Associate Director Arthur Kandel explained that some persons did not respond to the positive reinforcements of rewards and needed to devote "a certain period of time to what is known as negative reinforcers." These included "deprivation schedules"—loss of privileges as well as the old-fashioned prison punishment of solitary confinement in unlighted cells.

All men sent to Patuxent were given indeterminate sentences; they could be kept there until their behavior had been satisfactorily modified. Under these conditions, there was great pressure on the prisoners to conform to the behavior model favored by the Patuxent staff, whether or not they agreed with it. An anguished example of this pressure came to light at a meeting of the Patuxent Review Board, which passes on prisoners' applications for release. One applicant, Roosevelt Murray, had been confined in the prison for 14 years although his crime—car theft—initially involved only a four-year term. He had been diagnosed in Patuxent as sociopathic, had stabbed prison personnel and had consistently been denied freedom by the board. Murray told the 1972 hearing:

"You're killing me, aren't you? You people don't realize what you did to me in my 14 years here. You know that Roosevelt Murray never stabbed anyone before he came here. . . . If you had any decency, you'd let me go free. . . . Does it make any sense to hold me here when you see it isn't doing any good?"

The use of behavior modification at Patuxent and several other prisons in the United States has aroused public protest. Some institutions attempted to force prisoners into desirable behavior patterns with severe negative reinforcement—pain in one form or another. Drugs were used, including anectine, which makes the person feel that he is suffocating, and apomorphine, which induces prolonged vomiting. In a program called START (Special Treatment and Rehabilitation Training), the prisoner was confined to a solitary cell upon arrival at the prison; good behavior was required simply to enter normal prison life. Such inhuman programs have been attacked so vigorously that the U.S. government agency supporting them cut off funds for all behavior-modification experiments.

Less controversial results have been attained through the use of behavior modification in medicine and psychotherapy. Some treatment schemes employ negative reinforcement—electric shock, drugs—but since the patients generally accept treatment voluntarily and are free to quit whenever they please, punishments in this context seem less objectionable than in prison. Most programs, however, follow Skinner's techniques and depend entirely on rewards to induce changes in behavior.

On its simplest level, conditioning can sometimes relieve people of irrational fears. One of the most successful experiments was conducted by Albert Bandura, a psychologist at Stanford University. Bandura assembled 32 people affected by an uncontrollable fear of snakes, which interfered with their daily lives. Some were schoolteachers who panicked when pupils brought harmless pet snakes to their classrooms, others were Peace Corps volunteers who were being sent to snake-infested parts of the world and one was a woman who lived in terror because a neighbor kept a pet boa constrictor.

To desensitize these people, Bandura divided them into three groups. One group was shown films of snakes, the first scenes presenting snakes rather far off, the later ones portraying the feared reptiles closer and more clearly. The second group watched films of people handling snakes. The third group underwent a more radical regimen: after watching through a one-way mirror while a therapist played with a snake, the members of this group entered the room and eventually, encouraged to emulate the therapist, touched the snake and finally held it. This last treatment proved by far the most effective. At the end of 10 therapy sessions the members of group three could pass the ultimate test—each person let a snake crawl around on him for 30 seconds. The film treatments proved less effective, so Bandura later put the first two groups through the live snake-handling procedure; all were eventually cured of their fears.

Bandura's method of helping people overcome snake phobia parallels the operant conditioning of animals. Bandura's subjects were first introduced to a snake seen at a distance and thus gradually helped over a threshhold of fear. This lessening of their phobia was itself the reward. Conditioned to that extent, they then saw the snake closer up, achieving a second small victory. This reward encouraged them to expect an additional reward if they tried the next stage. They did, entering the same room with the snake—and so on. Similar systematic conditioning—gradual changes in behavior, each small step marked by a psychological reward—is reported to work to eliminate other phobias, cure alcoholism and sexual deviation, even to help people break the smoking habit.

Behaviorial techniques have also been widely used in mental hospitals with impressive results. The method is simple: patients are rewarded with tokens every time they perform desired acts. Initially the desirable behavior may be basic—getting out of bed, shaving, getting dressed and appearing at breakfast might earn tokens. Patients who have sat lethargically all day in a rocking chair are paid a token to get up and watch a job being

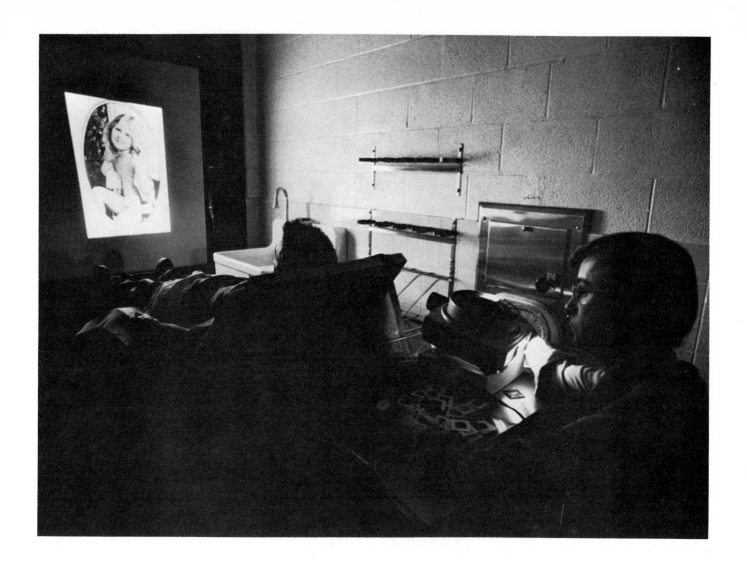

In one of the many uses of behavior-modification techniques to relieve personality aberrations, a man convicted of molesting children undergoes voluntary treatment in a Connecticut state prison. When the prisoner is shown a picture of a young girl, a psychologist (right) triggers a mild but unpleasant electric shock in an attempt to destroy the connection in the convict's mind between children and sexual pleasure.

done, and then more tokens for pitching in and helping. The point is that each desirable act is immediately reinforced with a tangible reward. The tokens earned are redeemable for special privileges that the patients consider attractive—permission to watch television, choice of a roommate, admission to a social event, a walk around the hospital grounds, even an afternoon trip into a nearby town.

These efforts sometimes produce dramatic results. In one hospital an elderly man had been so sunk in despair that he had refused to eat; for 15 years hospital attendants had force fed him to prevent starvation. After the token system was introduced he was soon putting a token in the cafeteria turnstile, picking up a tray, serving himself and eating a decent meal. Pioneers in the technique, psychologists Teodoro Ayllon and Nathan Azrin of Illinois' Anna State Hospital, started with 46 chronic schizophrenics and mental defectives. Soon after they had introduced the token economy, 30 per cent of the patients were able to earn tokens by working six hours a day as helpers in laboratories or offices. Eventually Ayllon and Azrin began to discharge some of their once-hopeless patients; within three years,

A cruise to lose
a stubborn habit

A unique experiment in changing behavior began on November 20, 1970, when 88 determined people set sail on a cruise ship bound for the Caribbean. They had decided to eradicate an ingrained pattern—smoking—and had 13 days in which to break the habit. The special cruise was organized by Dr. William Nemon, a psychiatrist who contends that it is easier to get rid of unwanted modes of behavior in pleasing new surroundings.

But just in case the relaxed shipboard surroundings failed to do the trick, a rigorous anti-smoking program was in effect on the cruise. Each day after breakfast there were films and lectures on smoking as a health hazard. This was followed by group meetings with psychologists at which the reasons for the tobacco addiction were discussed. After that came exercises in substituting deep breathing for smoking, and then a seminar on self-hypnosis as a tool to combat smoking. By putting themselves in a slight trance the smokers could divert themselves from the urge to smoke.

This indoctrination reduced smoking in the controlled environment on board ship, but the test came when the ship stopped at island ports and the passengers went ashore. As one of them described it, "Suddenly everyone we seé seems to be smoking, and we plunge into the shops to escape. The weakest-willed flee back to the ship."

At the end of the cruise, 80 per cent of the participants claimed to have broken the smoking habit. A follow-up study conducted six months later found that 37 per cent had succeeded in making this alteration in behavior at least relatively permanent.

Passengers on the stop-smoking cruise, confident of success, raise their hands in salute.

The cruise medical director, suggesting hypnosis to fortify the resolve of the habit breakers, teaches the passengers how to put themselves into a trance.

By sharing her feelings with her fellow smokers, a young woman explores her motivation for smoking and elicits help in reinforcing her desire to quit.

His wistful gaze riveted on a huge cigar in a shopwindow, a passenger fights temptation on a stroll around Curaçao, one of the cruise's ports of call.

21 of the original 46 patients were well enough to live outside the institution, in halfway houses, with their families or completely on their own.

Despite such apparent achievements through behavior modification, a number of psychologists—especially followers of Freud—question its true effectiveness. They believe the successes may be illusory. The overt behavior has been changed, they concede, but the original cause of the behavior defect has not been touched; they wonder how many discharged mental patients, for example, will eventually be forced to return to hospitals for further treatment. Exponents of the techniques respond that even a temporary cure is better than none.

The experts' criticism of the efficacy of behavior modification, however, is overshadowed by the doubts of those who think its benefits, if any, are outweighed by its perils. They are concerned not only about present and past uses of these techniques in prisons and for brainwashing, but even more about possible future use to control society. And they are hardly reassured by the statements of behavior modification's pioneer and chief propagandist, B. F. Skinner.

Skinner advocates the use of behavior modification to eliminate the ills of society, including war, pollution, overpopulation, injustice and every other imaginable evil. In fact, he is perhaps best known for his 1948 novel *Walden Two*, which describes a utopian community whose inhabitants have been so conditioned from birth that they want only what serves group interests. The community's fictional founder, Frazier, expresses Skinner's belief that humanity should establish a planned worldwide culture in which benevolent tyrants would use calculated rewards to make everyone behave in presumably desirable ways. Man, argues Frazier, is a mere machine whose behavior is as simply predicted and controlled as a chemical reaction in a test tube; the idea of an inner self with feelings, purposes, creativity and some capacity to take charge of its own destiny is held to be no more than myth or superstition.

Skinner's novel, along with a nonfiction version of it called *Beyond Freedom and Dignity* that he wrote in 1971, has been widely read—and just as widely disagreed with. His grand—not to say grandiose—vision of the future has been denounced by philosophers and scientists and has made him the most controversial contemporary figure in behavioral science. To detractors, his scheme is unworkable, potentially dangerous and morally wrong. They fear that the supposedly benevolent despots in Skinner's perfect society might decide to use punishment instead of reward to enforce demands; Skinner believes the rulers would not, since in Skinner's view punishment is ineffective in the long run. Equally troublesome is the question of who would decide what is good for society. Someone would have to play God. Frazier of *Walden Two*, admittedly Skinner's alter ego, speaks of a "point of similarity" between himself and God, and elsewhere says with a smile, "perhaps I must yield to God in point of seniority."

The strongest criticism of Skinner's utopia is that it seems grounded in an autocratic philosophy. Existential psychoanalyst Rollo May believes that Skinner is a totalitarian without quite realizing it. "I have never found any place in Skinner's system for the rebel," says May, "yet the capacity to rebel is of the essence in a constructive society." Skinner's response to such charges of authoritarianism: "If you insist that individual rights are the *summum bonum*, then the whole structure of society falls down."

Harvard social psychologist Herbert Kelman sums up the fears of his colleagues by observing: "For those of us who hold the enhancement of man's freedom of choice as a fundamental value, any manipulation of the behavior of others constitutes a violation of their essential humanity, regardless of the 'goodness' of the cause that this manipulation is designed to serve." Expressing it more succinctly, Richard Rubenstein, Professor of Religion at the University of Florida, observes that Skinner's "utopian projection is less likely to be a blueprint for the Golden Age than for the theory and practice of hell."

Behavior modification in its many forms and all the many other pressures today impose a heavy burden on the individual in his effort to retain his individuality. The growing bigness of everything—population, government and business bureaucracy, society's building scale—tends to dwarf his stature and minimize his worth. His identity is steam-rollered by forces ordaining conformity.

The logical—or rather illogical—extension of this anti-individual trend was described by Aldous Huxley in his *Brave New World*. It is a nightmare society where every facet of life—from test tube procreation through "dying rooms" with Muzak piped in—is rigidly ordered. Emotions that might give vent to individual expression are blunted by drugs providing instant joy and the state removes the daily anxieties of life by making all the decisions. A character called the Savage has grown up on an outer Reservation, exposed to the rigors of everyday existence and free to develop his own personality. When he is introduced to the programed environment of the central society, he rebels against its blandness and lack of challenge. The society's Controller says:

"We prefer to do things comfortably."

The Savage replies:

"But I don't want comfort. I want God, I want poetry, I want real danger, I want freedom, I want goodness. I want sin."

"In fact," says the Controller, "you're claiming the right to be unhappy."

"All right then," says the Savage defiantly. "I'm claiming the right to be unhappy."

The long trail in search of the Individual leads finally to this "savage" natural desire in all people: to strive during their lifetimes to develop fully the potential that is born in them; to experience all the emotions that the range of human existence has to offer; and always, above all else, to be permitted to become the individual that *their* hearts and minds tell them they should be.

Bibliography

*Also available in paperback.
†Available in paperback only.

Psychology

Adler, Alfred, *The Practice and Theory of Individual Psychology.* Humanities Press, Inc., New York, 1971.

Adler, Gerhard, and Aniela Jaffé, eds., *C. G. Jung Letters,* 2 vols. Bollingen Series, Princeton University Press, 1973.

Allport, Gordon W.:
Becoming. Yale University Press, 1955.
Pattern and Growth in Personality. Holt, Rinehart & Winston, Inc., 1961.

*Anastasi, Anne, *Individual Differences.* John Wiley & Sons, Inc., 1965.

†Barron, Frank, *Creative Person and Creative Process.* Holt, Rinehart & Winston, Inc., 1969.

Butcher, H. J., *Human Intelligence: Its Nature and Assessment.* Harper & Row Publishers, Inc., 1968.

*Chess, Stella, Alexander Thomas and Herbert G. Birch, *Your Child Is a Person.* Viking Press, Inc., 1972.

Cronbach, Lee J., *Essentials of Psychological Testing,* 3rd ed. Harper & Row Publishers, Inc., 1970.

*Davie, Ronald, and Neville R. Butler, *From Birth to Seven.* Humanities Press, Inc., 1972.

Erikson, Erik H., *Childhood and Society.* W. W. Norton & Co., Inc., 1950.

*Evans, Richard I., *Gordon Allport: The Man and His Ideas.* E. P. Dutton & Co., Inc., 1970.

Freud, Sigmund:
The Interpretation of Dreams, Basic Books, Inc., 1955.
On Creativity and the Unconscious. Harper & Row Publishers, Inc., 1958.

Gesell, Arnold, *The First Five Years of Life.* Harper & Row Publishers, Inc., 1940.

*Ghiselin, Brewster, ed., *The Creative Process.* University of California Press, 1952.

Hall, Calvin S., and Gardner Lindzey, *Theories of Personality.* John Wiley & Sons, Inc., 1970.

Hudson, Liam, *Contrary Imaginations: A Psychological Study of the Young Student.* Schocken Books, Inc., 1966.

Jones, Ernest, *The Life and Work of Sigmund Freud,* 3 vols. Basic Book's, Inc., 1957.

Jung, C. G.:
The Archetypes and the Collective Unconscious, in *Collected Works,* Vol. 9, Part I. Princeton University Press, 1959.
Man and His Symbols. Doubleday & Co., Inc., 1969.
Memories, Dreams, Reflections. Pantheon Books, Inc., 1963.

Kluckhohn, Clyde, and Henry A. Murray, eds., *Personality in Nature, Society and Culture.* Alfred A. Knopf, Inc., 1961.

Koch, Helen L., *Twins and Twin Relations.* University of Chicago Press, 1966.

Lehman, Harvey C., *Age and Achievement.* Vol. 33, Memoirs Series, Princeton University Press, 1953.

Maslow, Abraham H.:
The Farther Reaches of Human Nature. Viking Press, Inc., 1971.
Toward a Psychology of Being. Van Nostrand Reinhold Co., 1968.

McGuire, William, ed., *The Freud/Jung Letters. The Correspondence between Sigmund Freud and C. G. Jung.* Bollingen Series, Princeton University Press, 1974.

†McKim, Robert H., *Experiences in Visual Thinking.* Brooks-Cole, 1972.

Mischel, Harriet N., and Walter Mischel, *Readings in Personality.* Holt, Rinehart & Winston, Inc., 1973.

Murray, Henry A., et al., *Explorations in Personality.* Oxford University Press, 1963.

Mussen, Paul H.:
ed., *Carmichael's Manual of Child Psychology,* 3rd ed. John Wiley & Sons, Inc., 1970.
The Psychological Development of the Child. Prentice-Hall, Inc., 1963.

Rogers, Carl R., *Becoming Partners: Marriage and Its Alternatives.* Delacorte Press, 1972.

Schachtel, Ernest G., *Experiential Foundations of Rorschach's Test.* Basic Books, Inc., 1966.

Scheinfeld, Amram, *Twins and Supertwins.* J. B. Lippincott Co., 1969.

*Spock, Benjamin, *Baby and Child Care.* Simon and Schuster, Inc., 1973.

Stone, Joseph L., and Joseph Church, *Childhood and Adolescence,* 2nd ed., Random House, Inc., 1957.

Sullivan, H. S., *The Interpersonal Theory Of Psychology.* W. W. Norton & Co., Inc., 1953.

Thorndike, Robert L., and Elizabeth Hagen, *Measurement and Evaluation in Psychology and Education.* John Wiley & Sons, Inc., 1969.

Tyler, Leona E., *The Psychology of Human Differences.* Appleton-Century Crofts, 1965.

†Vernon, Philip E., *Intelligence and Cultural Environment.* Methuen & Co., Ltd., 1970.

Whyte, Lancelot Law, *The Unconscious Before Freud.* Doubleday & Co., Inc., 1962.

Wiggins, Jerry S., *The Psychology of Personality.* Addison-Wesley Publishing Co., Inc., 1971.

Yankelovich, Daniel, and William Barrett, *Ego and Instinct: The Psychoanalytic View of Human Nature.* Random House, Inc., 1970.

General

*Baines, Jocelyn, *Joseph Conrad: A Critical Biography.* McGraw-Hill Book Co., 1960.

*Benedict, Ruth, *Race: Science and Politics,* rev. ed. Viking Press, Inc., 1959.

Clark, Ronald W., *Einstein: The Life and Times.* World Publishing Co., 1971.

Dobzhansky, Theodosius, *Mankind Evolving, The Evolution of the Human Species.* Yale University Press, 1962.

Goertzel, Victor and Mildred, *Cradles of Eminence.* Little, Brown & Co., 1962.

Koestler, Arthur, *Insight and Outlook.* Peter Smith, 1967.

†Lyons, Nathan, ed., *Photographers on Photography.* Prentice-Hall, Inc., 1966.

Perruchot, Henri, *Gauguin.* World Publishing Co., 1964.

*Russell, Francis, *Tragedy in Dedham: The Story of the Sacco-Vanzetti Case.* McGraw-Hill Book Co., 1971.

Acknowledgments

For the help given in the preparation of this book the editors are especially indebted to Richard Wolf, Associate Professor of Psychology and Education, Columbia University, New York City, and also wish to thank the following individuals and institutions: Doris Albrecht, Kristine Mann Library of the Analytical Psychology Club of New York; Jack and Jeanne H. Block, Institute of Human Development, University of California at Berkeley; Anne B. Dolan, The Louisville Twin Study, University of Louisville School of Medicine; Robert N. Emde, Colorado Psychiatric Hospital, Denver, Colorado; Fred Ephraim, Huntington, N.Y.; Michael Lewis, Infant Lab, Princeton Educational Testing Service, Princeton, N.J.; Adam P. Matheny, The Louisville Twin Study, University of Louisville School of Medicine, Louisville, Kentucky; William J. Nemon, New York City; Mr. and Mrs. Bobby Parks and family, Louisville, Kentucky; James Ricks, Jr., Associate Director, Test Division, The Psychological Corporation,

New York City; Louise Riffenburgh, Rights and Permissions, The Psychological Corporation, New York City; Edwin Robbins, M.D., and Lillian Robbins, Ph.D., New York City; Lloyd Shewchuk, American Health Foundation, New York City; George Stricker, Institute of Advanced Psychological Studies, Adelphi University, Garden City, N.Y.; James M. Taylor, Jr., T. T. Knight Middle School, Louisville, Kentucky; Hiroshi Wagatsuma, Professor of Sociology and Anthropology, University of Pittsburgh, Pittsburgh, Pa.; Ronald S. Wilson, The Louisville Twin Study, University of Louisville School of Medicine, Louisville, Kentucky. *Pages 68-69:* Sample question 1 from the Scholastic Aptitude Test, Educational Testing Service. Reprinted by permission of the publisher. Sample questions 2, 6, 7 from the Lorge-Thorndike Intelligence Test, Verbal Battery, Level 4, Form B, © 1954.

Picture Credits

The sources for the illustrations in this book are shown below. Credits from left to right are separated by semicolons, from top to bottom by dashes.

Cover—Dan Budnik from Woodfin Camp and Associates. 6—Duane Michals. 10, 11—Ken Ohara. 14—The Bettmann Archive. 16—Ken Heyman. 17—Chris Bonington from Woodfin Camp and Associates—Fred Mayer from Woodfin Camp and Associates. 19—Edward Lear. 20—Bill Ray, TIME-LIFE Picture Agency, © 1972 Time Incorporated. 22—The Bettmann Archive. 23—Johann C. Lavater. 24—Scala, courtesy Museum of Fine Arts, Ghent. 26 through 37—Charles Harbutt from Magnum. 38—Erik Borg. 42—Edwin and Lillian Robbins. 44—Anthony Wolff. 45, 47—Esther Bubley. 48—Guido Mangold, courtesy *Eltern.* 49—Jay Maisel—Linda Ferrer Rogers. 52—James Barker. 54—Wendi E. Lombardi—Dena. 55—Max Dellacher. 58—© International Business Machines. 61—Copyright © 1937 James Thurber, copyright © 1966 Helen Thurber from *Thurber & Company,* published by Harper & Row, originally printed in *The New Yorker.* 64, 65—Thomas Gladwin; From "Native Astronomy in the Central Carolines" by Ward H. Goodenough, published by The University Museum, University of Pennsylvania—Thomas Gladwin. 67—William Bascom. 70—Courtesy Georgette and Géraldine Binet. 75—Signal Corps photo no. 111-SC-386 in the National Archives. 80—Pierre Orin. 82—Harvey Stein. 86

Reproduced by special permission of the publisher. Sample questions 3 and 5 from the Otis-Lennon Mental Ability Test, © 1967, by Harcourt Brace Jovanovich, Inc. Reproduced by special permission of the publisher. Sample questions 4, 8, 10, 12 from the Differential Aptitude Test, Form S, © 1972. Reproduced by permission of The Psychological Corporation, New York City. All rights reserved. Sample questions 9 and 11 from the Cureton Multi-Aptitude Test, Form B, © 1955. Reproduced by permission of The Psychological Corporation, New York City. All rights reserved. Sample question 13 from SRA Primary Mental Abilities Test for ages 5 to 7, © 1953 by Thelma Gwinn Thurstone and L. L. Thurstone, reproduced by permission of Science Research Associates, Inc. *Page 76:* Sample questions 1, 2, 4 taken from the Differential Aptitude Test, Form L, © 1972. Reproduced by

—Copyright © Mark Haven—Mark Silber, Dimension, Inc. 87—N. R. Farbmann, TIME-LIFE Picture Agency, © 1972 Time Incorporated—David F. Powers from Jeroboam. 90—Jon Brenneis; Ernest Stout—Cornell Capa from Magnum, courtesy TIME-LIFE Picture Agency, with permission of Grandma Moses Properties, Inc., New York. 91—United Press International—Rejlander, courtesy Gernsheim Collection; Culver Pictures. 92—Unosuke Gamo. 94, 95—Aaron Siskind; Edward Weston, printed by Cole Weston; William A. Garnett. 97—Left, "Beware of Imitations" by A. E. Brown and H. A. Jeffcott Jr., published by The Viking Press; right, collection of J. J. Lynx. 100, 101—David Douglas Duncan. 104, 105—Ralph Crane, TIME-LIFE Picture Agency, © 1972 Time Incorporated. 106—Ugo Mulas. 107—Copyright © Sherry Suris. 108—Suzanne Szasz. 109—Mary Ellen Mark. 110, 111—Dan Budnik from Woodfin Camp and Associates. 112, 113—Ken Heyman. 114—Cecil Beaton. 118, 121—The Bettmann Archive. 124—Drawings by Paul Good—Al Freni, reproduced by permission from the Block Design Subtest of the *Wechsler Adult Intelligence Scale.* Copyright © 1955 by the Psychological Corporation, New York, N.Y. All rights reserved—Courtesy Hans Huber Verlag, Bern, Switzerland. 128, 129—Courtesy Mrs. E. L. Freud; René Basset, Lyon. 134, 135—Courtesy Mrs. E. L. Freud. 136—From *Interpretation of Dreams* by Sigmund Freud (fourth through seventh editions), published by Basic Books, Inc. except top courtesy Mrs. E. L. Freud. 137—Bulloz, courtesy Musée du Louvre. 138

permission of The Psychological Corporation, New York City. All rights reserved. Bias question 3 taken from the Cooperative School and College Ability Test, reprinted by permission of Educational Testing Service, the copyright owner. Bias-free question 5 taken from Raven's Advanced Progressive Test. Set II, © John C. Raven 1962. Reprinted by permission of the Executors of the late John C. Raven. *Page 103:* quote from *Rose Where Did You Get That Red?* by Kenneth Koch. © 1973 by Kenneth Koch. By permission of Random House, Inc. *Pages 130-132:* quote from *Obedience to Authority* by Stanley Milgram. © 1974 by Stanley Milgram. By permission of Harper & Row, Publishers. *Pages 162-163:* quote from *Nineteen Eighty Four* by George Orwell. © 1949 by Harcourt Brace Jovanovich Inc. Reprinted by permission of Brandt and Brandt.

—Dmitri Kessel, TIME-LIFE Picture Agency, © 1972 Time Incorporated—© Glen S. Heller. 139—© Escher Foundation, The Hague—Goethe Museum; Erich Lessing, courtesy Naturhistorisches Museum, Vienna. 140—Courtesy Mrs. Gordon Allport—Fernand Bourges, TIME-LIFE Picture Agency, © 1972 Time Incorporated, courtesy Associated American Artists and Cincinnati Art Museum, Edwin and Virginia Irwin Memorial. 141—John Freeman, courtesy British Museum; Harvard University News Office. 142—John Wood; Picasso, Pablo. *Girl before a Mirror.* 1932. Oil on canvas, 64 x 51¼". The Museum of Modern Art, New York. Gift of Mrs. Simon Guggenheim. 143—Ted Polumbaum—Copyright Colorphoto Hans Hinz, Bâle, courtesy collection Ida Chagall. 144—Wide World Photos—Paulus Leeser, courtesy Mrs. John Koch. 145—Scala, courtesy Galleria Palatina, Palazzo Pitti, Firenze—Clemens Kalischer. 146—© Jill Freedman. 150—Doubleday. 154—Louis Courteville from TOP; Courtesy Sirot Collection—From *Gauguin* by Henri Perruchot, published by The World Publishing Company, 1963; The Minneapolis Institute of Arts. 157—Al Freni. 158—Thomas D. McAvoy, TIME-LIFE Picture Agency, © 1972 Time Incorporated. 163—Ken Heyman for *Time*—Yale Joel, TIME-LIFE Picture Agency, © 1972 Time Incorporated. 164—Loomis Dean, TIME-LIFE Picture Agency, © 1972 Time Incorporated. 166—Ernie Hearion, *The New York Times.* 168, 169—Bill Ray, TIME-LIFE Picture Agency, © 1972 Time Incorporated.

Index

*Numerals in italics indicate a photograph
or drawing of the subject mentioned.*

X Printed in U.S.A.